SALAMANCA TRAVEL GUIDE 2023

Explore Salamanca: Comprehensive guide to planning your trip to Salamanca, Spain 2023 and beyond

Jennifer C. Webber

TABLE OF CONTENT

Map of Salamanca

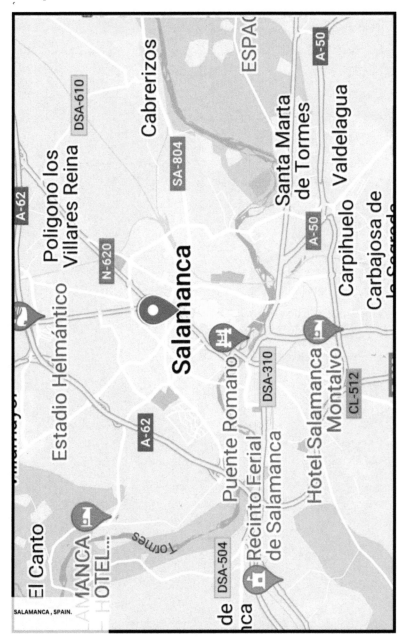

INTRODUCTION

Welcome to Salamanca, a bustling Spanish city located in the center of the country. Salamanca, known for its extensive past, stunning architecture, and esteemed university, charms visitors with a unique fusion of antiquated allure and contemporary vitality. You will be surrounded by a patchwork of centuries-old customs, breathtaking landmarks, and a thriving cultural environment as you meander through its winding alleyways.

Salamanca has a long history that goes back to Roman times, and it has long been a center of learning and culture. The University of Salamanca, one of the oldest universities in Europe and a UNESCO World Heritage Site, is the city's finest achievement. This prestigious institution has drawn academics, thinkers, and artists from all over the world, helping to establish the city's image as a hub of learning.

Salamanca's architecture is beautiful in every way. The "Golden City," the city's historic core, is a mesmerizing collection of magnificent structures and monuments that incorporate Romanesque, Gothic, Renaissance, and Baroque architectural elements. The renowned Plaza Mayor, the center of Salamanca, is regarded as one of Spain's most attractive squares thanks to its opulent facades and lively ambiance.

Walking through Salamanca's streets is like entering a real-life museum. Whether it's the beautifully carved façade of the Salamanca Cathedral, the antiquated Roman Bridge over the Tormes River, or the lovely House of Shells ornamented with its distinctive scallop shells, every corner of the city tells a fresh tale. The city is a photographer's dream and a must-visit location for history buffs because of its beautiful architecture and rich history.

Salamanca is more than just a city stuck in the past, though. The thousands of students that reside there renew its youthful spirit, bringing life, innovation, and a thriving nightlife to the streets. The city's student population makes sure it is vibrant and energetic all year long with a variety of cultural events, live music shows, and busy tapas bars where you can enjoy the flavors of Castilian cuisine.

Salamanca delivers an entire experience that will amaze you, whether you're meandering through the charming lanes, admiring the breath-taking landmarks, or indulging in the regional cuisine. This travel book will be your dependable travel companion while you explore Salamanca's attractions. It offers insider advice, in-depth knowledge, and a wealth of suggestions to make your trip to Salamanca an experience you won't soon forget. Prepare to travel through time and culture as we uncover Salamanca's treasures, Spain's undiscovered gem.

History

The city's strategic location along the Tormes River made it a hub of commerce and trade, attracting settlers and paving the way for its eventual transformation into a thriving cultural center. Salamanca's roots run deep, dating back to ancient times when it was a Roman settlement known as "Salmantica."

Salamanca prospered under Moorish authority in the Middle Ages until being regained by the Christian kingdom of León in the 11th century. The city expanded dramatically during this time as it rose to prominence as a major religious hub, home to numerous magnificently constructed monasteries and cathedrals that dot the surrounding countryside.

The famed University of Salamanca was founded in Salamanca in the 13th century, bringing the city international acclaim. After its 1218 founding, the university swiftly rose to prominence as one of the continent's top centers of learning, drawing academics from all around. It was crucial in the dissemination of knowledge, encompassing disciplines like law, theology, philosophy, and the sciences. The university's reputation for intellectual excellence attracted luminaries like Miguel de Unamuno, a well-known philosopher, and Francisco de Vitoria, a well-known name in international law.

During the Renaissance, Salamanca saw its heyday as a center of artistic and architectural success. With the erection of spectacular buildings that displayed a seamless fusion of Gothic, Plateresque, and Renaissance styles, the city's skyline underwent a dramatic transformation. During this prosperous time, famous buildings were built, such as the Salamanca Cathedral and the beautiful House of Shells, which are both known for their magnificent architecture and intricately decorated exteriors.

Salamanca had its glorious moments, but it also experienced times of adversity and instability. The city encountered difficulties throughout the Spanish Civil War and the Spanish War of Independence, leaving scars that are still noticeable today. While conserving its historical history and embracing a contemporary era of advancement and innovation, it emerged from these turbulent times with a revitalized energy.

Salamanca is a thriving city today that combines its famous past with a vivacious current. Its famous institution continues to draw students from all around the world, bringing a vibrant young culture to the streets. The city's historic center, which has been carefully kept and is listed as a UNESCO World Heritage Site, is proof of its lasting importance and alluring allure.

Everywhere you turn in Salamanca's streets, you'll see reminders of its colorful past. Salamanca welcomes tourists to immerse themselves in a tapestry of centuries-old traditions and amazing accomplishments. This tapestry is represented by the Roman Bridge that spans the Tormes River, a sign of the city's ancient beginnings, and the majesty of the Plaza Mayor, a tribute to its architectural brilliance.

Investigating Salamanca's past is like taking an enthralling trip through time. It is a city where the ascent and fall of empires, the quest for knowledge, and the tenacity of its inhabitants have all been seen. your travel book will join you on your exploration, helping you to understand the historical events, folklore, and landmarks that helped Salamanca become the amazing place it is today. As you enter a realm where the past and present harmoniously converge, get ready to be enchanted by Salamanca's fascinating history.

Traditions and Culture

Salamanca's thriving culture and extensive traditions produce a setting that is just as alluring as its incredible architectural wonders. A genuinely immersive experience is provided to tourists by the city's cultural tapestry, which brings together a variety of influences from its historical roots to its vibrant current environment.

Salamanca's cultural legacy has always been centered on music, art, and literature. Numerous writers and painters have used the city as their inspiration throughout the ages, producing works of incredible beauty and originality. Salamanca has established an environment that promotes artistic expression and intellectual investigation, from the poetic lines of Fray Luis de León, a renowned Spanish poet and professor, to the thought-provoking works of Miguel de Unamuno.

Salamanca's esteemed university has a big influence on the city's cultural landscape. The intellectual curiosity fostered by the academic community permeates the city and fosters lively debates, lectures, and conversations on a variety of topics. Salamanca is energized by the university's presence and has a dynamic cultural scene.

In Salamanca, local festivals and festivities are valued because they offer a window into the city's vibrant past. The Fiestas de la Virgen de la Vega, which honors the city's patron saint and is held in September, is one of the most well-known celebrations. The streets come to life with vibrant processions, upbeat music, and traditional dances, fostering a feeling of happiness and community. Along with having a distinct place in Salamanca's cultural calendar, Semana Santa processions draw both locals and tourists with their melancholy beauty.

Salamanca's culture is firmly rooted in the gastronomic arts and offers a mouthwatering culinary experience. Numerous bars and taverns in the city provide mouthwatering tapas dishes that are complemented with regional wines. Salamanca's gastronomic delights reflect the rich flavors of Castilian cuisine, with dishes like savory jamón ibérico and juicy chorizo as well as delicious cheeses and classic cocido.

Learning and language are fundamental to Salamanca's cultural heritage. The teaching of Spanish as a foreign language honors the city's rich linguistic legacy and draws students from all over the world who want to learn the language and experience the allure of the city. Beyond its renowned university, Salamanca is dedicated to education, offering immersion experiences in Spanish language and culture to those who are willing to study and appreciate it.

Salamanca also has a thriving theater, music, and dance scenes, with many venues and events displaying a wide variety of cultural activities. From classic plays to modern musicals, the Teatro Liceo, a historic theater from the 19th century, showcases a range of performances. The vibrant live music culture in the city provides a stage for regional and international performers to dazzle listeners with their skill in genres ranging from jazz and rock to classical and flamenco.

Salamanca's cultural legacy smoothly fuses tradition and modernity into everyday life. The city welcomes you to immerse yourself in its rich cultural tapestry by going on a gallery tour, taking in an exciting concert, or taking part in a traditional festival. In addition to offering insights and suggestions to help you fully appreciate Salamanca's distinctive charm and aesthetic attraction, this travel book will expose you to the city's lively culture and cherished traditions. Get ready to be mesmerized by Salamanca's cultural treasures as you explore a world where innovation, tradition, and creativity coexist.

Geography and climate

Salamanca is located in a beautiful environment that highlights the area's variety of natural beauties. The city is surrounded by the rich plains and undulating hills of the Castilla and León area, which is located in the western section of the nation.

Salamanca's historical development has been significantly influenced by its advantageous location along the banks of the Tormes River. The river flows through the nearby countryside, bringing a sense of calm to the city's setting. Salamanca's historic district and the verdant countryside on the other bank are connected by the Roman Bridge, an old architectural wonder that spans the Tormes River.

The geographic features of the city offer outdoor enthusiasts and nature lovers an intriguing backdrop. There are many chances for hiking, mountain biking, and exploring unspoiled natural landscapes in the surrounding Sierra de Francia mountain range with its rough terrain and stunning perspectives. River valleys and flowing streams in the area create quaint areas of peace that entice tourists to relax and take in the beauty of the surrounding landscape.

Salamanca has a Mediterranean climate with influences from the continent. Average summertime temperatures range from the mid-20s to the low-30s Celsius (mid-70s to low-90s Fahrenheit), and they are usually mild and dry. The summer months are the best time to explore the city's ancient streets and outdoor attractions because of the city's abundant sunshine.

Salamanca's winters are often chilly, with lows that are close to or just below freezing. Snowfall is nevertheless relatively infrequent, and the city frequently enjoys bright winter days. The city's architectural treasures take on a particular attractiveness against a background of a winter environment, giving the colder months a special beauty.

Salamanca is best visited in the spring and fall because of the warm weather. As flowers blossom and vegetation changes, the city comes alive with brilliant colors, giving its parks and streets a hint of enchantment. These times of year provide pleasant weather for outdoor activities and sightseeing in the city.

Geographically and climatically, Salamanca is a welcoming place that provides a range of activities all year long.

Salamanca's natural location adds to its attraction as an enticing tourist destination, whether you're strolling through its old streets in the warm summer sun, savoring the peace of the nearby countryside in the spring and autumn, or exploring the city's beauty in the winter.

You can take advantage of Salamanca's natural beauty and climate fluctuations by following the advice in this trip guide, which will give you insightful information. Prepare to be immersed in Salamanca's stunning topography and friendly atmosphere as you set off on a wonderful adventure through this alluring Spanish city, from seeing the city's architectural gems to exploring the nearby natural surroundings.

Why Visit to Salamanca

Salamanca draws tourists from near and far. There are several reasons why this alluring Spanish city should be at the top of your trip agenda.

The unrivaled architectural splendor of Salamanca is one of its key attractions. A collection of historical architectural treasures may be found in the city's historic core, which is a UNESCO World Heritage Site. Salamanca's architectural marvels will astound you, from the magnificent Salamanca Cathedral with its elaborate carvings and towering spires to the charming House of Shells with its symbolic scallop shells covering the façade.

One of the oldest universities in Europe, Salamanca's esteemed university adds a special depth to the city's allure. Salamanca has developed into a dynamic hub of study and innovation as a result of the university's long intellectual heritage and tradition.

Visitors will find themselves in a lively and interesting setting thanks to the youthful energy that the academic environment pumps into the streets. Salamanca's university offers an extra level of interest to your stay, whether you're taking a tour of the beautiful campus buildings, attending a lecture, or just taking in the intellectual atmosphere.

The cultural scene in Salamanca is a hidden gem just waiting to be discovered. Artists and creative thinkers from all over the world are drawn to the city because of its reputation as a center for literature, art, and music. Traditional and contemporary artworks are displayed in art galleries, while audiences are enthralled by performances in theaters and concert halls. Attend a live music show, check out an art gallery, or explore Salamanca's literary past to fully immerse yourself in the city's rich cultural tapestry.

You should not miss Salamanca's delectable cuisine. The city's famed tapas scene provides a delicious tour of the flavors of Spanish food. Salamanca's cuisine entices the taste senses with everything from traditional jamón ibérico and substantial cocido to delectable cheeses and beautiful pastries. Set off on a culinary trip by visiting several tapas bars, relishing the delectable nibbles, and becoming fully immersed in the lively social ritual of "going for tapas."

The geographic position of Salamanca lends the city additional charm. The city serves as a gateway to outdoor activities and natural beauty because it is surrounded by stunning landscapes and undulating hills. Discover the Sierra de Francia mountains nearby, go hiking on beautiful routes, or take a leisurely stroll along the Tormes River's banks. Salamanca's topography provides a tranquil break from the city's bustling streets, enabling you to commune with nature and appreciate the splendor of the nearby countryside.

Salamanca is known for its ethereal aura, which transcends time. Its old-world streets, thriving cultural scene, and intellectual legacy all work together to make for a fascinating vacation. Salamanca promises to engage your senses and leave an imprint on your trip through Spain, whether you're a history aficionado, an art lover, a foodie, or a curious traveler looking for new experiences.

You can depend on this travel guide to be at your side as you explore Salamanca. It will offer priceless insights, useful advice, and suggestions to make sure your trip is full with unforgettable events. Prepare yourself for an unforgettable journey through Salamanca's architectural marvels, intellectual heritage, cultural riches, culinary delights, and magnificent scenery. Learn what makes Salamanca such a popular tourism destination that visitors are encouraged to make repeated trips there.

CHAPTER 1

Making Travel Plans for Salamanca

Traveling to Salamanca gives you the chance to become fully immersed in the fascinating culture, rich history, and stunning architecture of this alluring Spanish city. Salamanca provides a multitude of experiences just waiting to be found, whether you're a history fan, an art enthusiast, or simply looking for a place filled with charm. Careful planning is essential for a seamless and memorable trip. Get ready to embark on an incredible trip as you explore Salamanca's stunning city.

Ideal Season to Visit

Depending on your tastes and the kind of experience you're looking for, you can choose the perfect time to visit Salamanca. You can customize your trip to suit your interests and aspirations by visiting throughout each season, which each has its own special charm and exploration opportunities.

Summer (June to August)

The months of June through August are prime travel season for Salamanca. Warm temperatures and lengthy daylight hours give the city a lively, dynamic feel. This time of year is perfect for taking leisurely strolls around Salamanca's colonial alleyways, relaxing at outdoor cafes, and getting fully immersed in the local arts scene. However, it's important to keep in mind that the summer months may be fairly crowded with tourists and that the temperature can occasionally soar higher. As a result, be ready for the odd crowd and think about finding shade during the hottest parts of the day.

Salamanca has a Mediterranean climate with influences from the continent. Salamanca experiences warm, dry summers with average high and low temperatures in the mid-20s to low-30s Celsius (mid-70s to low 90s F). The summer months are a desirable time to tour the city's historic streets because of the warm weather and longer days.

Autumn and spring

Salamanca's shoulder seasons, which bring beautiful weather and less tourists, are spring and fall. The city receives temperate temperatures from March to May and from September to November, which makes it a great time to explore its architectural marvels and surrounding landscapes.

The weather during these transitional times is typically nice, with lows in the 70s and highs in the mid-50s Celsius (mid-50s to low 20s Fahrenheit). Autumn charms with brilliant foliage, bringing a touch of natural beauty to the city's streets and parks, while spring provides colorful blooms and new vegetation. These times of year are best if you want a more laid-back and serene experience. You may immerse yourself in the culture, visit galleries and museums, and enjoy the gastronomic treats of the city at your own speed.

Winter (December to February)

From December through February, Salamanca experiences winter, which offers a unique view of the city. Despite occasionally being colder, the atmosphere is distinct because of the fresh air and sporadic sunshine. You may enjoy the city's architectural treasures in a tranquil setting throughout the winter because of the quieter, more intimate ambiance that winter offers.

Additionally, you can get the chance to participate in regional celebrations and events, including the Christmas markets, which will give your trip a magical touch. Just be sure to pack enough of warm gear and enjoy Salamanca's quaint winter atmosphere.

When making travel plans, it's crucial to take into account the regional celebrations and events. The calendar of Salamanca is filled with lively events that offer a rich cultural experience. For instance, the September Fiestas de la Virgen de la Vega festival features a beautiful display of processions, music, and dancing, letting you see the city's customs in action.

The serious religious ceremonies on display during the Semana Santa (Holy Week) processions, which take place in the spring, are a reflection of the city's rich history.

The city's academic calendar is another thing to consider. Numerous students are drawn to Salamanca's esteemed university, and throughout the academic year, the city is alive with youthful vitality. Visit Salamanca during the academic year for a unique experience full of intellectual conversations, cultural events, and a buzzing social scene if you prefer a lively and vibrant atmosphere.

However, scheduling your visit outside of term time may be more appropriate if you prefer a quieter atmosphere.

The ideal time to travel to Salamanca ultimately depends on your particular interests and the experiences you want to have. Take into account the weather, the number of people, and the kinds of activities that most interest you. Salamanca welcomes you with open arms, offering a memorable voyage through its enthralling history, culture, and architectural treasures, whether you're drawn to the vivacity of summer, the serenity of spring and autumn, or the quiet beauty of winter.

What to watch and read before a trip

Before you even arrive in this wonderful Spanish city, immerse yourself in the Salamanca atmosphere. You can increase your enjoyment and excitement for your approaching journey by reading books and viewing movies that highlight Salamanca's rich history, cultural legacy, and aesthetic allure. To spark your imagination and get you ready for the wonders that lie ahead, consider the following suggestions:

Books:

The work of Carlos Ruiz Zafón, "The Shadow of the Wind"

- This spellbinding book takes you on a literary odyssey through enigmatic libraries and well-kept secrets, weaving together love, mystery, and the power of literature. It is set in Barcelona but contains references to Salamanca.

Maira Duenas' "The Seamstress"

- This historical book takes you back in time as it describes the experience of a young seamstress during the Spanish Civil War. Salamanca's University and its thriving cultural scene are important to the plot and reveal some of the city's intellectual history.

By Lisa Marie Mercer, "Salamanca Revisited":

- Explore the author's personal experiences and reflections as she strolls through Salamanca's ancient neighborhoods, engages with the city's lively culture, and discovers its hidden jewels. This memoir offers a distinctive viewpoint on Salamanca's appeal and fascination.

Movies:

The Spirit of the Beehive, "El Espritu de la Colmena"

- This classic Spanish movie explores a young girl's infatuation with cinema and her quest for self-discovery while taking place in a distant community with ties to Salamanca. It perfectly encapsulates both the enchantment of movie and rural Spain.

Spanish Affair, "Ocho Apellidos Vascos":

- Although not specifically situated in Salamanca, this romantic comedy is set throughout Spain, including Salamanca. It provides a playful and amusing representation of Spain's cultural diversity and regional identities.

"The Oxford Murders"

- This suspenseful mystery-thriller, which is set in both Oxford and Salamanca, centers on a string of killings linked to intricate mathematical ideas. Salamanca is praised for its stunning architecture and status as a hub of intellectual activity in the movie.

You can obtain a deeper grasp of Salamanca's significance and become immersed in its atmosphere even before your trip thanks to the literary works and movies that will take you right into the city's history, culture, and creative ambience. Your enthusiasm for the voyage ahead will be increased as you read and listen about Salamanca's architectural marvels, intellectual legacy, and compelling charm.

Information Entry Requirements and Visa

It's essential to familiarize yourself with the visa rules and entry procedures before beginning your trip to Salamanca to ensure a simple and hassle-free visit. You can follow the instructions below to complete the essential stages and gain knowledge of the visa application process and related fees.

Entry Requirement

Travellers must meet different entry requirements depending on their nation of citizenship because Salamanca is in Spain. With a current national identity card or passport, citizens of the European Union (EU), European Economic Area (EEA), and Switzerland may enter Salamanca and the rest of Spain. Short-term visits do not require a separate visa.

If you are coming from a country other than the EU, EEA, or Switzerland, it is imperative to find out if you need a visa to enter Spain. Depending on your nationality, the reason for your travel, and the length of your stay, different visa rules may apply.

For the most recent and correct information regarding visa requirements, it is advised that you get in touch with the Spanish embassy or consulate in your home country or visit the ministry of foreign affairs' official website.

Cost of Visa

The cost of a visa for Salamanca varies based on your nationality, the kind of visa you need, and how long you plan to stay there. It's vital to check the current rates before applying because visa fees can change.

Consult the official website of the Spanish embassy or consulate in your country to get the most precise and comprehensive information on visa fees. The embassy or consulate will give you complete details about the particular visa type you require, the related costs, and the payment procedure.

Application Methodology

It's crucial to adhere to the instructions provided by the Spanish embassy or consulate in your country while applying for a visa to Salamanca. The procedure normally entails filling out an application form, supplying the necessary supporting documentation, including a current passport, evidence of lodging, a travel schedule, travel insurance, financial resources, and, if appropriate, a letter of invitation.

It is recommended to start the visa application procedure long before the dates of your desired travel to allow for processing. It's vital to make plans in advance because the processing times for visas can differ depending on your country of residence.

It's important to note that the information provided here should only be considered a general overview; for the most accurate and up-to-date information regarding entry requirements, visa fees, and the application process for Salamanca, please contact the official authorities or visa processing centers.

You may assure a pleasant trip to Salamanca and concentrate on taking in the city's attractive views, rich culture, and impressive heritage by becoming familiar with the entry criteria and visa procedures.

Exchange Rates and Money

When organizing your vacation to Salamanca, it is crucial to comprehend the local currency and conversion rates. An easy and convenient financial experience during your vacation will be made possible by having a firm understanding of the financial system and knowing where to exchange your money. Here are some tips to help you understand Salamanca's money system:

The Euro (€) is Spain's official currency. It is generally recognized in all businesses in Salamanca, including hotels, eateries, retail stores, and other spaces. For minor transactions, it is important to have some cash on hand because some tiny establishments could only accept cash.

You can exchange your currency for Euros in Salamanca at a number of sites, including banks, exchange offices, and designated currency exchange kiosks. Banks typically provide competitive exchange rates, however they could also charge extra fees and have restricted hours. Alternative choices include exchange offices and kiosks, which frequently have handy locations in tourist regions and operate for longer hours.

To be sure you're getting the greatest deal, it's a good idea to compare exchange rates and fees before exchanging your money. Remember that exchange providers' rates may range slightly from one another. It's also a good idea to find out if there will be any additional fees, such as commissions or service fees.

Salamanca is dotted with automatic teller machines, or "cajeros automáticos" as they are known in Spanish. They offer a practical option to get cash directly from your bank account in euros. It's a good idea to check with your bank in advance because you should be aware that there can be fees associated with foreign withdrawals.

In Salamanca, credit and debit cards are generally accepted, especially in bigger establishments. The most widely accepted cards are Visa and Mastercard, with American Express and Discover perhaps having a smaller acceptance range. To ensure easy use of your cards when traveling, it's a good idea to let your bank know about your intentions. You should also ask about any foreign transaction fees or daily withdrawal limits.

For flexibility, it is essential to carry both cash and cards. Although cards make transactions easier, keeping some cash on hand is helpful for modest purchases like snacks or trinkets from neighborhood markets.

Although Salamanca is usually thought of as a safe city, it is always advisable to use caution when handling money and valuables. Use safe ATMs, keep an eye on your possessions, and keep big amounts of cash hidden from view.

You can manage your funds successfully when visiting Salamanca if you are familiar with the local currency, exchange rates, and payment alternatives. To guarantee a trouble-free and pleasurable financial experience in this fascinating Spanish city, keep in mind to plan ahead, check prices, and notify your bank of your vacation plans.

Visitor Stay Permit

It's crucial to be informed of the rules governing your stay in Spain before organizing your trip to Salamanca. To remain lawfully in Salamanca, you might need to obtain a visitor's stay permission, sometimes known as a "residence permit" or "tourist visa," depending on your nationality, the reason for and length of your visit.

A seamless and legal stay will be made possible by being aware of the prerequisites and processes for acquiring a stay permit.

Here are some tips that will help you:

Duration of Stay

- You may typically stay in Salamanca for up to 90 days without a stay permit if you are a citizen of a nation that is a member of the European Union (EU) or the Schengen Area. This holds true for short-term travel, business trips, and other objectives. You might need to apply for a stay permit prior to your arrival if you want to remain longer or if you are a citizen of a nation that is not in the European Union or the Schengen Area.

Visa Requirement

- Before visiting Salamanca, visitors from a number of nations outside the EU or the Schengen Zone must apply for a tourist visa. The standard visa application procedure entails providing the necessary paperwork, including a current passport, a filled-out application form, evidence of travel insurance, proof of lodging, and enough money to cover your stay. It's crucial to confirm the precise visa requirements and application procedures with the Spanish embassy or consulate in your country of residence.

Application Process

- It's advised to start the application procedure well in advance of your intended trip if you want a stay permit. Depending on your nationality and the reason for your visit, the application procedure could change.

- The Spanish embassy or consulate will often require you to submit an application form, together with any necessary supporting documentation, fees, and maybe an interview. It's crucial to carefully follow the embassy or consulate's instructions and to give correct and thorough information.

Extending Your Stay

- It could be possible to request for an extension or change of status if you are currently in Salamanca and want to stay longer than is permitted. Typically, this procedure entails filing an application to the appropriate Spanish authorities. To make sure you take the right steps and fulfill the requirements, you should get legal counsel or assistance from the relevant immigration authorities.

Adherence to Regulations

- As soon as you arrive in Salamanca, it's crucial that you follow the guidelines on your stay permission. You must also adhere to the stated reason for your visit, the permitted length of your stay, and any other conditions or restrictions listed on your permit. Failure to abide by these rules may result in fines, deportation, or difficulty when traveling to Spain in the future.

It's important to be aware that depending on your nationality, the reason for your travel, and current immigration laws, the particular requirements and processes for getting a stay visa may change. For the most accurate and recent information relevant to your case, it is advised to check official sources like the Spanish embassy or consulate.

You can guarantee a lawful and stress-free stay in Salamanca by being aware of the procedures and requirements for guest stay permits there. To make your trip to Salamanca interesting and pleasurable, keep in mind to prepare early, obtain the required paperwork, and get advice from the appropriate authorities.

CHAPTER 2

Getting to Salamanca

Travellers from both domestic and foreign locations can reach Salamanca with ease because to the city's excellent transit connections. Salamanca is easily accessible by plane, train, or picturesque road trip, depending on your preferred mode of transportation.

By Air

Air travel is frequently the most effective and time-saving method of getting to Salamanca from faraway locations. Matacán Airport (SLM), which is ideally located 15 kilometers from the city center, provides convenient service to the area. Although Matacán Airport primarily handles domestic flights, there are a few international connections that enable visitors from different parts of the world to access it.

Depending on the airline you choose, the season, and the departure city, the cost of flying to Salamanca can change. To get the greatest deals, it's a good idea to compare prices and get your tickets in advance. Additionally, search for more economical solutions by considering flexible trip dates.

There are various ways to get to Salamanca's city center after landing at Matacán Airport. Taking a taxi is one of the easiest options. At the airport, taxi services are easily accessible, offering a straight and hassle-free transfer to your destination.

Taxi

Depending on variables including the time of day and the precise location of your destination inside Salamanca, the approximate cost of a taxi from Matacán Airport to Salamanca can range from [€100-€200].

It's important to keep in mind that taxi prices can fluctuate, so it's best to find out the current prices at the airport taxi stand or from the driver before starting your trip. Taxis are frequently metered, and the cost is determined by the distance covered.

Bus

Budget-friendly options include public buses, whose itineraries coincide with airplane arrival times.

Since a bus can be taken immediately from the airport, this is the simplest choice.

Average time from airport to Salamanca town: 2 hours and 45 minutes

Cost price: €30 one way or €55 round trip

Buses are provided Monday through Friday from 9 am to 11.15 pm and on Saturday and Sunday from 1 pm to 9.15 pm. For timetables and reservations, go to www.avanzabus.com. Phone: +34900921895

Train

You must travel to the Estación de Chamartn in order to board a train; you can do this by taking the metro or a taxi.

Average time: 2.5 to 3 hours

Price: €30 one-way or €60 round-trip

Between 8.45 am and 9.30 pm, trains run.

For timetables and reservations, visit www.renfe.com

How far is the airport from Salamanca?

The metro ride takes around 21 minutes and travels a distance of about 15 kilometres from Madrid Airport (MAD) to Salamanca. The Madrid Airport (MAD) to Salamanca subway service, run by Metro de Madrid, departs from Aeropuerto T-4 and arrives in Nuevos Ministerios.

The best way to get from London to Salamanca is to train which takes 15 hours and 55 minutes and costs between £300 and £650. Alternatively, you can take the bus, which takes 27h 15minute and costs between £200 to £330.

By opting to travel quickly and conveniently to Salamanca, you may start your exploration of this lovely Spanish city with ease. To ensure a smooth arrival at Matacán Airport, remember to plan ahead, think about your travel options, and get yourself ready. Taxi services and other transportation alternatives will be easily accessible to take you to your destination in Salamanca.

By Train

Train travel is a great option if you want to reach Salamanca in a scenic and leisurely manner. Salamanca is easily reachable from many areas of Spain because to its well-connected rail system, which lets you travel in luxury while admiring the alluring Spanish scenery.

You can count on Renfe, Spain's national train company, to deliver effective rail services as you set off on your train excursion to Salamanca. Regular train service from Renfe connects Salamanca with a number of significant cities, including Madrid, Barcelona, Seville, and more. The Salamanca train station is conveniently situated in the heart of the city, ensuring a smooth transition whether you're coming from inside Spain or arranging an overseas connection. www.renfe.com

The price of a rail ticket to Salamanca might change based on a number of variables. The cost of the ticket may vary depending on the route taken, the service level selected, and the train type. Renfe has a variety of rail alternatives, including fast AVE trains for short trips and regional trains that let you take in the surrounding scenery. Due to their shorter journey durations and superior comfort, high-speed trains typically cost a little bit more than regional trains.

It is advised to check the Renfe website or speak with a travel agent if you want reliable and current information about train timetables and ticket costs. It is advised that you purchase your tickets in advance because doing so not only guarantees their availability but also enables you to benefit from any potential discounts or special offers, particularly during periods of high travel demand.

You have a number of options for getting to your destination after you arrive at the Salamanca train station. Taxis are easily accessible right outside the train station if you want an easy and quick transport. In Salamanca, taxi services are dependable and offer a hassle-free ride that will take you directly to your lodging or any other preferred destination inside the city.

When taking a taxi, it's a good idea to tell the driver where you're going and ask how much the trip should cost before you leave. The taxi rate will vary depending on the route taken, the time of day, and any applicable extra fees or taxes.

Buses and trams, which provide reasonably priced ways to get to many Salamanca locations, are also available close to the train station if you want to take public transit. While traveling the city, these public transit options offer the possibility to fully experience the local culture.

By taking the train to Salamanca, you may experience a relaxing and pleasant journey while taking in the beauty of the Spanish countryside. Whether you want to take a high-speed train or prefer the slower tempo of regional services, Spain's railway network offers a dependable and pleasurable mode of transportation to get you to this charming city. Taxis and other transportation options will be easily accessible when you arrive at the Salamanca train station to guarantee a smooth continuation of your vacation.

By Bus

The bus is an excellent alternative if you're looking for an easy and economical method to go to Salamanca while taking in the beautiful scenery along the way. Due to its excellent transport connections, Salamanca can be reached from many towns within Spain and even from nearby nations.

You can depend on various bus operators that run frequent routes to Salamanca to start your bus adventure there. Businesses like ALSA, Avanza, and Socibus provide dependable and comfortable bus services, guaranteeing a pleasurable journey.

The price of a bus trip to Salamanca can change depending on the distance, level of service, and bus company you choose. The cost of the tickets is typically less expensive when compared to other forms of transportation, making it a desirable choice for tourists on a tight budget. For precise and current information on timetables and ticket costs, it is advised to check the websites or get in touch with the bus companies directly.

You will typically arrive at the Estación de Autobuses, Salamanca's major bus terminal, which is conveniently located inside the city. If your lodging is close by, you may even be able to reach different areas of Salamanca on foot from there by using the local public transportation system.

When you arrive at the bus station, cabs are easily accessible outside and provide a simple option to get to your destination in Salamanca if you would prefer a more direct transfer. In Salamanca, taxi services are dependable and the drivers are typically knowledgeable with the city's tourist hotspots. It's a good idea to tell the taxi driver where you're going and ask how much the estimated fee will be before you start your trip to prevent any unpleasant surprises.

By traveling about Salamanca by bus, you may experience the local culture and take in the scenery. It is a reasonable choice with flexibility in terms of departure times and routes. The wide bus network makes it easy for you to get to this fascinating Spanish city, whether you're coming from a nearby city or from a more remote place.

When you decide to take a bus to Salamanca, you may start a pleasurable journey while taking in the varied scenery along the way and anticipating learning more about the city's rich history, culture, and charm.

How to navigate Salamanca itself

Walking

- It takes about 30 minutes to walk from one side to the other. Walking is a fantastic choice because the town is small and all of the services, stores, and attractions are near by.

- It is simple to stroll around, take in the sights, and savor the ambience in the town center because the majority of it is pedestrianized.

Buses

- Salamanca has its own bus network, With a total of 13 bus lines that operate daily between the hours of 7.15am and 11.45pm.

- Additionally, there are night buses that operate from 11.30 p.m. to 3 a.m. (or 4 a.m. on Thursday, Friday, and Saturday).

- One trip costs €2, however you can save money by buying a bus card for a predetermined number of trips.

Taxis

- The average cost of a taxi ride from one side of town to the other is between €5 and €15.

Station information

- The bus terminal is situated on the Avenida de Filiberto Villalobos, northwest of the town's core.
- Salamanca's train station is called Vialia, and it is located in Paseo de la Estación.

Cycling and Foot Travel

- The ease with which you may get around Salamanca on foot or by bike is one of the wonderful things about visiting. Salamanca welcomes you to immerse yourself in its wonderful atmosphere and discover its hidden gems at your own leisure thanks to its small size and pedestrian-friendly streets.

The most entertaining and practical method to go around Salamanca is probably by foot. The ancient district of the city is small and simple to navigate, enabling you to wander along its cobblestone lanes and take in the architectural marvels that surround you. You'll come across the city's rich history and vibrant culture at every turn as you stroll through the Plaza Mayor, the majestic churches, and the bustling squares.

You may find quaint cafes, boutiques, and local businesses tucked away in Salamanca's little lanes by exploring the city on foot. You can take leisurely stops to savor mouthwatering Spanish food, enjoy a cup of fragrant coffee, or engage in some people-watching as the city comes to life all around you.

Bike tours are a great way to discover Salamanca because they are both somewhat faster and more environmentally friendly. For cyclists of all abilities, the city has a well-developed infrastructure for cycling, including designated bike lanes and trails, making it safe and fun. There are many places to hire bicycles, and they come in all shapes and sizes. Traditional bikes, electric bikes, and even guided bike tours are available if you want something more regimented.

You may easily travel further and get to sites that are a little outside of the city center by hopping on a bike. Salamanca's beauty can be enjoyed while taking a pleasant break from the city's hustle by pedaling along the riverbanks or through the green parks.

You'll enjoy Salamanca's pedestrian-friendly layout and the simplicity with which you may discover its riches whether you decide to tour the city on foot or by bicycle. Each stride or pedal stroke will lead you to new discoveries and unforgettable experiences, from the architectural treasures to the colorful plazas and cultural sites.

As you go out on your Salamanca walking or bike excursion, keep in mind to wear comfortable shoes, dress for the weather, and drink enough of water. Though getting lost in the city's picturesque streets can also be part of the fun, keep a map or navigation app close at hand.

So, lace up your walking shoes or mount your bike and set out on a riveting tour of Salamanca's enchanting streets. Exploring Salamanca by foot or by bike enables you to genuinely connect with the city's character and make lasting memories of your trip, whether you decide to wander around the city's historical core or peddle along the picturesque pathways.

CHAPTER 3

Top Salamanca Attractions

S alamanca is home to numerous major attractions that draw tourists from all over the world. This fascinating city provides a variety of activities that will captivate your senses and leave you in awe. Salamanca has plenty to offer everyone, whether you're a fan of art, history, or simply want to immerse yourself in a distinctive atmosphere.

We will delve into Salamanca's greatest attractions in this guide, so be ready to travel through time and beauty as we uncover the treasures that make Salamanca a must-visit location.

New Salamanca Cathedral

The New Cathedral, or Catedral Nueva, rises majestously in the center of Salamanca and is a magnificent example of Gothic and Renaissance design. This magnificent building, which was constructed between the 16th and 18th centuries, is one of the city's most recognizable features and a must-see destination for tourists.

Address: Plaza de Juan XXIII 4, 37008 Salamanca, Spain.

What to see

- Prepare to be astounded by the New Cathedral's majesty and minute intricacies as you approach it. With exquisite carvings and decorative ornamentation, the facade exhibits a remarkable fusion of Gothic and Plateresque styles. Take a moment to see the beautiful sculptures and fine stones that decorate the exterior.

- You'll be greeted by a stunning interior when you enter. A large nave with vaulted ceilings and imposing columns extends before you. The vivid hues of light that are reflected from the stained glass windows produce a spellbinding ambiance. Make sure to glance up to view the exquisite altarpiece and the finely carved choir seats, both of which are classic Renaissance masterpieces.

- Explore the several chapels, each of which features a distinctive architectural style and contains important artwork, as you make your way further into the cathedral. The Chapel of San Martn, which features excellent frescoes, and the Chapel of the Immaculate, which is embellished with colorful tilework, are not to be missed.

Things to do

- There are a number of things you may do to make your experience at the New Cathedral more enjoyable. To learn more about the cathedral's history, significance as a building, and the tales behind its stunning artwork, think about taking a guided tour. Some excursions even grant visitors access to places that are off-limits, giving them a rare opportunity to see the cathedral's undiscovered gems.

- Attending a mass or other religious ceremony can be an unforgettable way to connect with the cathedral's sacred environment for those seeking a spiritual experience. An atmosphere of true awe is created by the organ's reverberation and the harmonies of the choir voices echoing across the vast room.

Tips for touring

1. Here are some suggestions to remember in order to get the most out of your trip to the New Cathedral:

2. Choose a less busy time to visit to avoid heavy crowds. Weekdays or early mornings are often less busy.

3. Consider the cathedral a place of worship and dress appropriately. It is advised to wear modest clothes that covers your knees and shoulders.

4. To make the most of your time exploring Salamanca, think about getting a combo ticket that provides entry to additional adjacent sights including the Old Cathedral and the Clereca Tower.

5. Explore at your own pace and take everything in. Pay attention to the fine details of the carvings, the way the light catches the stained glass windows, and the way the architectural features have been designed.

Insights

The New Salamanca Cathedral is a symbol of the community's rich artistic and cultural history. Its lengthy construction process produced a distinctive combination of architectural styles that work in harmony to produce a truly spectacular building. The cathedral's importance goes beyond its position as a place of worship because it also acts as a living memorial to Salamanca's past and a representation of the city's talent in the arts and architecture.

A trip through time and art may be had by visiting the New Cathedral, where you can take in Salamanca's rich spiritual and cultural heritage while admiring the intricate craftsmanship of the past.

In the New Cathedral, where history, art, and spirituality come together to create an extraordinary experience, be prepared to be in wonder as you go through the doors. Take your time to take in its magnificence, marvel at the minute details, and take in the meditative atmosphere that permeates this amazing architectural masterpiece.

Nearest hotels to the cathedral

---

1. Eurostars Las Claras Hotel

The New Cathedral is conveniently close to the Hotel Eurostars Las Claras, which is located in Salamanca's historic district. This contemporary hotel offers chic accommodations, a pleasant ambiance, and a comfortable lounge area. You'll have quick access to not only the New Cathedral but also other landmarks, eateries, and retail establishments thanks to its strategic position.

Address: Calle Marquesa de Almarza s/n, 37001, Salamanca, Spain

Distance: 0.3 Miles from new cathedral

Contact: +34923128500

Cost price for various rooms per night:

1. Double or twin room: $96

2. Double room with parking: $110

3. Single room: $90

There are categories of these rooms with different prices.

NOTE: Price varies

Popular features

No cost WiFi

Breakfast is offered

Conditional air

Commercial service

In-room dining

Parking is accessible

---

2. Hotel Hospes Palacio Hotel de San Esteban

This opulent hostel is housed in a gorgeously refurbished 16th-century monastery and is close to the New Cathedral and the University of Salamanca. Enjoy the exquisite setting, roomy accommodations, and first-rate amenities, which include a spa and a rooftop pool with stunning city views. In close proximity to the New Cathedral, the Hotel Hospes Palacio de San Esteban offers a very unique stay.

Address: Lugar Arroyo Santo Domingo 3, 37008, Salamanca, Spain

Distance: 0.3 Miles from new cathedral and 8 miles from matacan airport

Contact: +34923262296

Cost price for various rooms per night:

1. Deluxe double room: $320

2. superior double room: $274

3. Junior suite: $360

There are categories of these rooms with different prices.

NOTE: Price varies

Popular features

No cost WiFi

Breakfast is offered

Conditional air

Commercial service

In-room dining

Parking is accessible

Conference facilities

Car hire

Outdoor swimming pool

Airport shuttle

Map of Salamanca New Cathedral

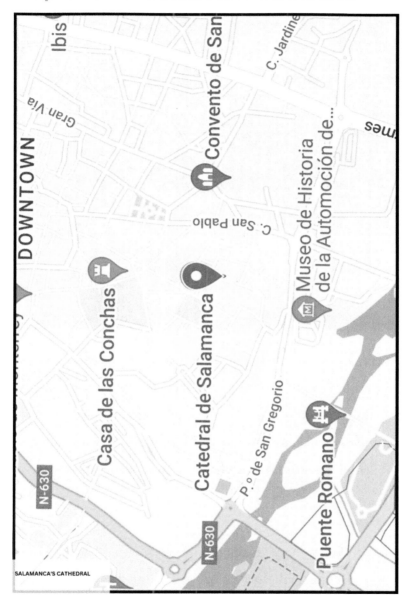

Leronimus

Salamanca's old University Library, known as Leronimus, is a tribute to the city's rich intellectual history and a source of information. This 16th-century architectural marvel provides a fascinating look into the world of academia and the lengthy history of Salamanca's esteemed university.

What to see:

- Prepare to be taken to a previous era of learning and intellectual endeavor as soon as you enter Leronimus. The gorgeous interior of the library boasts spectacular vaulted ceilings, towering shelves filled with antiquated books, and intricate woodwork that exemplifies historical craftsmanship. Spend a moment admiring the intricate features and taking in the academic ambiance that permeates the area.

- The library's collection is a veritable gold mine of information, including priceless historical records, rare manuscripts, and antiquated publications. Among the highlights are priceless publications like the Polyglot Bible and the Beatus Commentaries. Admire the exquisitely illuminated pages and deft calligraphy, and you'll have a greater understanding of the skill and commitment that went into creating these literary gems.

Things to do

- Leronimus offers more than just a visual feast during a visit. To enhance your experience and delve further into the academic world, you can take part in a variety of events. Consider going on a guided tour, which will be given by knowledgeable professionals who may share fascinating details about the library's past, present, and important works. You might even be given access to restricted places during some excursions, allowing you to explore undiscovered nooks and obtain a deeper understanding of the library's significance.

- Leronimus frequently holds cultural gatherings, exhibits, and talks that honor contributions to literature, history, and academia. To see whether there are any special events that coincide with your visit, check the library's calendar. Attending a lecture or exhibition can give you a fresh viewpoint and further acquaint you with Salamanca's intellectual tradition.

Tour guide

Here are some ideas to keep in mind in order to get the most out of your trip to Leronimus:

- Plan your visit in advance and confirm the library's hours of operation because access may be restricted or limited at particular times.

- Be aware of the guidelines established by the library. Avoid touching the books or upsetting the sensitive items in the peaceful environment.

- You should be careful to adhere to any rules or limits that may be in place regarding photography.

- To make the most of your time in the city, think about combining your visit to Leronimus with taking in other local sights including Salamanca's historic center and the university buildings.

Leronimus is more than just a library; it is a tangible illustration of the value of education and the lasting impact of Salamanca's academic tradition. It maintains a major role in the history of intellectual endeavors as one of the first universities libraries in Europe. The library's extensive collection and stunning architecture serve as a tribute to the university's commitment to learning and scholarship.

You can engage with the intellectual spirit that has characterized Salamanca for ages by visiting Leronimus. It is a chance to see how history, art, and academia all come together in a place that has fostered the brains of innumerable intellectuals and philosophers throughout history.

Enter Leronimus now to begin your adventure through the history of knowledge. Allow the opulence of the library, the calm of the reading rooms, and the profound sense of history that permeates the space to enthrall you. You will have a greater understanding of the intellectual traditions that have formed Salamanca and left a lasting impression on the academic community by immersing yourself in this center of learning.

Address: Plaza juan XXIII, s/n, 37003 Salamanca, Spain
Phone Number: +34923266701
Website: www.ieronimus.es

Hotels close to Lerominus

1. Hotel Alda rio torme

Address: Av Salamanca, 1, 37900 santa marta de tormes, Salamanca, Spain

Distance: 0.2 Miles from new cathedral

Contact: +3492399113

Cost price for various rooms per night:

It varies according to room type you needed.

Popular features

No cost WiFi

Breakfast is offered

Conditional air

Airport shuttle

Commercial service

In-room dining

Parking is accessible

Car hire

Outdoor swimming pool

Universidad de Salamanca

One of the oldest colleges in Europe, the Universidad de Salamanca, proudly stands as a beacon of academic brilliance and aesthetic beauty. This esteemed institution, founded in the 13th century, never ceases to awe and excite tourists with its fascinating past, magnificent structures, and scholarly legacy.

What to see

- An opportunity to see the University of Salamanca's amazing architectural treasures and get a fascinating look into the past are provided by a visit. Start your tour with the impressive Plaza de Anaya, where the university's main facade is awe-inspiring in its elaborate Plateresque design. Admire the intricate features on the façade, such as the carved figures, coats of arms, and religious motifs.

- The Patio de las Escuelas, a wonderful courtyard surrounded by exquisite Renaissance and Baroque buildings, should be visited. Admire the exquisite reliefs and figures on the Escuelas Mayores' façade and the neighboring Escuelas Menores' magnificent Plateresque design. Take a time to admire the harmonious coexistence of the university's many architectural eras.

- Visit the historic university libraries, which include a sizable collection of rare books and manuscripts, like the Biblioteca General Histórica and the Biblioteca de la Universidad. Explore the magnificent lecture halls that have hosted great academics and students for ages. They feature exquisite ceiling decorations and historical antiques.

What to do

There are various things you may do to maximize your time at the Universidad de Salamanca while exploring it:

1. Get a tour guide:

- Take a tour to see the university's rich past, stunning buildings, and famous alumni. The academic accomplishments and cultural significance of the university will be discussed in detail by knowledgeable advisors.

2. Visit a lecture or event of culture:

- For information about lectures, performances, exhibitions, and other cultural events, consult the university's calender. You can get a taste of the lively intellectual and creative atmosphere that permeates the institution by attending one of these events.

3. Visit the university's museum:

- Discover the Salamanca University Museum, which includes a varied collection of antiquities, works of art, and historical items that highlight the university's illustrious history. Learn more about the history of the institution and how it influenced Salamanca's cultural environment.

Tour guide:

Take into account the following advice to make your visit at the Universidad de Salamanca rewarding and enjoyable:

1. Put on some relaxed shoes:

- Because the university complex is huge and you'll be walking a lot, you should wear comfortable shoes.

2. Verify the opening times:

- Verify the opening times of the many structures and libraries that make up the university complex because they can operate on different schedules.

3. Respect the academic setting:

- Keep in mind that the university is a place for learning and research, so act appropriately by being quiet and without touching or moving any books or artifacts.

4. Visit in the morning or evening:

- Consider visiting the university early in the morning or late in the day to avoid crowds and truly take in its majesty.

Insights:

The Universidad de Salamanca, which has fostered the brains of luminaries in academics for centuries, has a major place in the history of learning. Since its inception, it has served as a hub for knowledge and intellectual interaction, drawing students from all over the globe.

One cannot help but be overwhelmed by the overwhelming sense of history that permeates the campus as they walk through its revered halls. The Salamanca University has been a part of crucial times in the history of knowledge, generating ground-breaking discoveries and encouraging the development of innumerable brilliant minds.

The university's lasting legacy is still present.

to develop Salamanca's reputation as a cultural and educational hub. It acts as a bustling center for academics, researchers, and students to collaborate and explore new areas of knowledge.

The Salamanca University has an impact outside of academia. Its magnificent architecture, which combines Gothic, Renaissance, and Baroque styles, is a reflection of the city's extensive architectural history. Ornate façades, grand courtyards, and elaborate sculptures all serve as reminders of the creative and intellectual triumphs that have thrived there.

The university has also served as a gathering place for brilliant minds throughout time. It has received important individuals who have made a lasting impact on the fields of literature, philosophy, and law such as Miguel de Unamuno, Francisco de Vitoria, and Antonio de Nebrija. Students and academics are still motivated by their presence and intellectual achievements today.

Beyond its historical significance, the Salamanca University is now a thriving hub for learning and research. It draws students from all over the world who want to immerse themselves in the intellectual environment and uphold the traditions of this distinguished institution since it offers a wide choice of academic programs.

When you visit the Universidad de Salamanca, you get the chance to engage with centuries of intellectual curiosity, invention, and scholarly endeavors in addition to exploring gorgeous structures and ancient treasures. It enables us to comprehend the significant influence that education and information may have on society and future generations.

Take a time to think about the innumerable brains that have entered this renowned institution, the concepts that have been developed in its lecture halls, and the tremendous influence it continues to have on the academic community as you stroll the hallways and take in the ambience.

The Salamanca University is a tribute to the value of education, intellectual rigor, and the quest for knowledge. Visits to this prestigious institution provide an incredible voyage through history, culture, and intellectual brilliance that leave a lasting impression on everyone who has the opportunity to do so.

Address: Plaza de fray luis de leon 1-8, 37008 Salamanca' Spain

Phone number: +34923294418

E-Email: internat@usal.es

Website: www.cursosinternacionales.es

Nearby hotel

1. **Los Angeles plaza**

For tourists looking to relax and unwind, this hotel provide excellent amenities. A guest can take advantage of well-equipped fitness centre to maintain his or her workout routine while traveling.

Address: Plaza Mayor. 10, Salamanca, 37002. Salamanca, Spain

Distance: 0.4km from Salamanca University

Contact: +34923218166

Cost price for various rooms per night:

1. Twin Room with Private External Bath: $44

2. Triple room with shared Bathroom: $55

3. Family room with shared Bathroom: $60

There are categories of these rooms with different prices.

NOTE: Price varies

Popular features

No cost WiFi

Breakfast is offered

Conditional air

Commercial service

In-room dining

Parking is accessible

Conference facilities

Casa de las Conchas

Casa de las Conchas, a beautiful architectural jewel tucked away in the center of Salamanca, with an unusual façade embellished with hundreds of scallop shells. This unusual structure, which dates to the late 15th century, welcomes visitors to learn about its history, take in its beauty, and unearth its secrets.

What to see:

- Get ready to be mesmerized by Casa de las Conchas' striking facade as you approach. Over 300 carefully carved and arranged sandstone shells, totaling over 300, are used to embellish the façade, producing an amazing work of art.

- Take a moment to ponder the amazing symbolism that these shells symbolize, the minute intricacies, and the delicate interaction of light and shadow.Explore the interior of the house by going inside to discover a secret patio that exudes serenity. A magnificent center fountain, elegant columns, and a gallery with a cloister-like ambiance all embellish the courtyard. Enjoy this secret paradise' tranquility and charm by taking a leisurely stroll.

- Explore the building's interior further to find the hidden riches. As a public library, the Casa de las Conchas offers a haven for books and information. Browse the shelves, explore the library's collection of books and manuscripts, and take in the scholarly ambiance that surrounds this historic location.

Things to do:

- Consider participating in the following activities to improve your experience while at Casa de las Conchas:

Take a tour guide:

- Explore the past and significance of Casa de las Conchas by taking a guided tour. The construction of the building, its distinctive architectural elements, and the intriguing legends surrounding it will all be explained by knowledgeable guides.

Participate in cultural events:

- Check the calendar for any cultural events that might be held at the Casa de las Conchas, such as art exhibits, book readings, or musical performances. These occasions give you the chance to become fully immersed in the neighborhood's artistic community and to take in Salamanca's vibrant cultural offers.

Enjoy some time for thought:

- Choose a quiet area of the courtyard or one of the reading rooms, and take time to relax and reflect. Consideration and introspection are encouraged by the Casa de las Conchas's serene atmosphere and historical significance.

Tips for touing:

Here are some suggestions to help you get the most out of your time at Casa de las Conchas:

Make a visit plan:

- Plan your visit based on the Casa de las Conchas' operating hours. To properly appreciate the building's beauty and peace, think about going when it's more quiet.

Respect the space:

- Because Casa de las Conchas is a place with cultural significance, always act respectfully. Reduce the amount of noise you make and refrain from touching any exhibits or objects on display.

Behold the beauty:

- Bring your camera if you want to record the distinctive architectural elements and keep your memories of Casa de las Conchas since photography is permitted in most places of the building.

Insights:

More than just a stunning piece of architecture, Casa de las Conchas serves as a representation of Salamanca's illustrious past, rich culture, and pursuit of knowledge. The shells on the building's façade have several symbolic meanings, including the journey to Santiago de Compostela and the previous owner's illustrious ancestry. They are evidence of the diverse influences and artistic styles that have defined Salamanca over time.

You can connect with Salamanca's spirit of exploration, learning, and artistic splendor by going to Casa de las Conchas. It serves as a reminder of the city's standing as a hub of intellectual brilliance and a proof of the cultural riches' lasting attractiveness.

You'll be taken back in time as you tour Casa de las Conchas, taking in a variety of architectural styles and historical significance. The structure's conversion from a private home to a public library illustrates how it has evolved and changed over time, securing its history as a beloved cultural icon.

Intriguing tales are also contained within the Casa de las Conchas. According to legend, the shells were added to the façade to hide hidden treasures. Even if the reality of this story is still a mystery, it gives the building's already alluring atmosphere a magical touch.

In addition to its stunning architecture, Casa de las Conchas is a haven for learning. Within its premises, a public library welcomes guests to browse the volumes in its holdings, developing a love of reading and a better appreciation of Salamanca's intellectual history. Both locals and visitors can congregate here to immerse themselves in the world of literature, seeking comfort and motivation among its shelves.

Casa de las Conchas captures the spirit of Salamanca with its harmonious fusion of art, history, and literature. It represents the city's dedication to safeguarding its cultural gems and developing areas where the past and modern may peacefully coexist. The opportunity to enter Salamanca's lively cultural landscape, where the search of knowledge and the love of beauty merge, is extended by a visit to this architectural wonder.

May you experience a strong sense of gratitude for the intellectual and historical legacy that Casa de las Conchas represents as you leave, taking with you the memories of its charming façade, secret courtyard, and literary riches. Salamanca's ongoing fascination is attested to by the Casa de las Conchas, which invites inquisitive minds to explore, contemplate, and develop a deep appreciation for the cultural treasures that characterize this alluring city.

Address: Calle Compania, 2, 37002 Salamanca, Spain.
Timings: 9.00am-9.00pm
Phone: +349232269317

Nearby Hotel:

Hotel Alda Rio Tormes

This hotel has a seasonal outdoor pool, tennis court, a spa and free Wi-Fi zone. It is located next to El Tormes Shopping centre, 2km from Salmanca's historical centre. The bed room are well decorated with good furniture and well carpeted floor.

The hotel is located 5mins drive from the beautiful town of Salamanca centre, including the cathedral and Salamanca's university.

Economy Double Room

Beds: Two single bed

Price per night: $47

2. Double or Twin Room

Beds: Two single bed

Price per night: $55

There are many other rooms available so you make a choice.

Address: Av. Salamanca, 1, 37900 Santa Marta de Tormes, Salamanca, Spain.

Phone: +34923999113

Museo de la Casa Lis Art Nouveau y Art Deco

A hidden gem in Salamanca, Museo Art Nouveau and Art Deco Casa Lis transports tourists to the alluring realm of early 20th-century art and design. This one-of-a-kind museum offers a look into an age characterized by elegance, inventiveness, and artistic expression through its amazing collection of Art Nouveau and Art Deco treasures.

What to see:

- As you enter the Museo Casa Lis, get ready to be mesmerized. A dazzling variety of decorative arts, including fine glasswork, delicate jewelry, fashionable furniture, and elegant sculptures, are featured in the museum's expertly organized exhibits. Admire the exquisite details, vivid colors, and supple curves that characterize the Art Nouveau and Art Deco movements.

- The museum's outstanding collection of stained glass is one of its centerpieces. The rooms are bathed in a kaleidoscope of light thanks to the radiant panels, whose intricate patterns and vivid colors add to the splendor of the displayed artworks.

Things to do:

- To improve your experience while browsing Museo Casa Lis, think about doing the following things:

Get a tour guide:

- Join a guided tour to learn more about the historical setting and artistic trends of the exhibits. The artists, their methods, and the cultural influences that influenced the Art Nouveau and Art Deco movements will be revealed by knowledgeable guides.

Participate in a seminar or lecture:

- For workshops or talks on subjects linked to Art Nouveau and Art Deco, check the museum's program. You can gain a deeper understanding of the artworks by participating in these interactive events, which also provide an opportunity to learn more about the artistic methods and craftsmanship used at the time.

Take a break in the museum café:

- While you're taking a break from exploring, unwind in the museum's café. Enjoy a wonderful croissant or a cup of coffee while taking in the museum's opulent atmosphere. It's the ideal setting for thinking back on the amazing works of art you've seen.

Tips for touring:

- Here are some suggestions to help you get the most out of your trip to Museo Casa Lis:

- Confirm the museum's opening times before your visit to make sure you have enough time to take your time and examine the exhibits.

photographing tips:

- While taking pictures in museums is typically permitted, you should be aware of any particular rules or regulations put in place to safeguard the artwork. As you photograph the beauty of the exhibitions, stay away from flash and be mindful of other guests.

Take your time:

- Due to the size of the museum's collection, allow enough time to thoroughly appreciate the artwork and take in its fine nuances. Allow yourself to be mesmerized by the works of art on show and to admire the skill that went into making them.

Insights:

The Art Nouveau and Art Deco trends, which transformed the art world in the early 20th century, are visible through the lens of Museo Casa Lis. The collection offers a window into the cultural transformations and artistic breakthroughs of the time by showcasing the inventive designs and forward-thinking aesthetics that appeared throughout this changing age.

The museum offers a venue for appreciation and interchange of cultures in addition to preserving and displaying these great works of art. It encourages a deep respect for the artistry and craftsmanship of the creators who embraced these ground-breaking trends, making a lasting impression on the field of design.

Consider the influence of the Art Nouveau and Art Deco styles on the development of aesthetics, design, and daily life as you walk through the magnificent hallways of Museo Casa Lis. Allow the artworks' beauty and sophistication to take you back in time. where the bounds of inventiveness were stretched.

Beyond its function as an art archive, Museo Casa Lis is significant. It also acts as a center for culture, presenting touring exhibits, educational events, and other activities that help people learn more about the Art Nouveau and Art Deco movements. The museum offers a lively and engaging experience, with everything from lectures by subject-matter experts to interactive workshops that let you try your hand at making art inspired by the time.

Museo Casa Lis offers important insights into the socioeconomic, technological, and aesthetic advancements that influenced the Art Nouveau and Art Deco periods through its collection and programming. It demonstrates how these trends pushed away from the past and embraced a bold and forward-looking style by emphasizing the blending of traditional craftsmanship with cutting-edge materials and processes.

You may admire the creativity, workmanship, and cultural influence of Art Nouveau and Art Deco by visiting Museo Casa Lis. You are encouraged to examine the minute intricacies of each item, to be in awe of its beauty and grace, and to learn more about the artistic vision that gave rise to an entire era.

You'll get a fresh appreciation for the past artistic accomplishments as you lose yourself in the museum's atmosphere, surrounded by the luxurious furnishings and mesmerizing artworks. The Art Nouveau and Art Deco art movements' ageless beauty and ingenuity are celebrated at Museo Casa Lis, which is a tribute to their ongoing attractiveness.

A trip to the Museo Art Nouveau and Art Deco Casa Lis guaranteed to be fascinating and educational, regardless of whether you are an experienced art fan or are just interested in the aesthetic legacy of the early 20th century. Allow the treasures contained inside its walls to inspire and stoke your own artistic soul as you get ready to be transported to a world where creativity and aesthetics ruled supreme.

Address: Gibraltar, 14, 37008 Salamanca, Spain
Timings: 11am-7pm
Phone: +34923121425
Distance: 0.3 miles from Salamanca centre

Map of Museo de la Casa Lis Art Nouveau y Art Deco

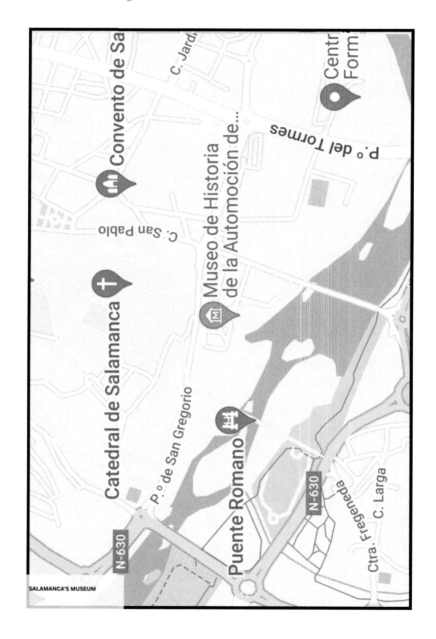

Puente Romano

The Puente Romano, or Roman Bridge, is a monument to Salamanca's extensive historical past. This historic bridge, which spans the placid waters of the Tormes River, gives tourists the chance to travel back in time and take in the engineering wonders of the Roman Empire.

What to see:

- Take a moment to examine Puente Romano's enormous stone arches and solid craftsmanship as you approach it. With its substantial stone blocks and sophisticated design, the bridge's well-preserved construction exemplifies the inventiveness of Roman engineering.

- You can enjoy expansive views of the surrounding area from the bridge, including the charming riverbanks and the alluring Salamanca cityscape. Capture the bridge's beauty as it reflects in the Tormes' glistening waters, creating a captivating scene.

Things to do:

- To improve your experience when exploring Puente Romano, think about doing the following things:

Go for a leisurely stroll:

- Enjoy the peace of the bridge by strolling quietly across its historic arches. Take in the atmosphere as you go across the bridge and consider how many people's feet have walked along this important route over the years.

Enjoy the beautiful scenery:

- Take some time to enjoy the beautiful scenery as you go down the bridge. Experience the tranquil ambience of this ancient site while admiring the river's and its environs' natural beauty.

Taking unforgettable pictures

- Bring your camera or smartphone if you want to take beautiful pictures of Puente Romano. Whether it's the bridge itself, the river, or the distant metropolis, the bridge provides a myriad of gorgeous photo opportunities.

Tips for touring:

Here are some suggestions to help you get the most out of your trip to Puente Romano:

Visit when it's more quiet:

- Consider visiting the bridge off-peak hours if you want to truly feel the atmosphere and have a more tranquil experience. Avoiding crowds and relishing the serene beauty of the surrounds are best accomplished in the early morning or late afternoon.

Put on some relaxed shoes:

- Keep in mind that Puente Romano entails walking across a historic bridge with uneven surfaces while you explore it. Choose comfortable shoes that will make navigating the stone pathways simple.

Combined with surrounding sights:

- The Old Cathedral and the Plaza Mayor are just a few of the popular sites that are conveniently placed close to Puente Romano. For a thorough investigation of Salamanca's historical gems, think about scheduling your stay to include these adjacent attractions.

Insights:

Puente Romano provides a window into the Roman presence in Salamanca during its early years and the lasting effects of their engineering prowess. It illustrates the relationship between the past and the present and acts as a reminder of the city's rich legacy.

It's impossible to avoid feeling in awe of and regard for earlier generations while crossing Puente Romano. This historic bridge experienced the ups and downs of history as it passed through its arches with many travelers, traders, and troops. It stands tall as a link across eras and represents the tenacity and endurance of human accomplishments.

The bridge's basic structure hasn't altered throughout the years, despite restoration and maintenance efforts. Puente Romano is a physical reminder of the magnificence and sophistication of ancient civilizations, acting as a bridge to the past.

A trip to Puente Romano offers the ability to interact with history and appreciate the extraordinary craftsmanship of the Romans in addition to appreciating its stunning architecture. It provides a chance to pause and contemplate time's passage and the enduring legacy of human creativity.

Allow yourself to be engulfed by the weight of history as you cross the Roman Bridge. Consider the significance of this historic building and the tales its stones might convey if they could talk. Imagine the trade caravans, the military marching, and the footsteps of regular people going about their everyday lives that once filled this bridge with humming activity.

Puente Romano offers a special vantage point from which to see Salamanca's surrounding natural beauties. You are enticed to pause, take in the fresh air, and savor the tranquility of the moment by the harmonized backdrop provided by the serene flow of the Tormes River beneath the bridge.

You'll learn as you explore Puente Romano that the site's historical and cultural significance goes beyond the building itself. It acts as a symbolic link between the past and the present, serving to remind us of the enduring legacies that have shaped our world.

Consider the tenacity of this historic architectural wonder as you stand on Puente Romano. The bridge has endured the test of time and the difficulties it has encountered while patiently observing Salamanca and its inhabitants' development.

A trip to Puente Romano is essential whether you're a history or architecture enthusiast, looking for a quiet place to take in Salamanca's splendor, or none of the above. In order to connect with the rich fabric of human history and be inspired by the creativity of those who came before us, it delivers an immersive experience that transcends time.

Take your time to take in the ambience, enjoy the historical significance, and consider the tales that this bridge has silently borne down the ages as you cross Puente Romano's age-old stones. Let it serve as a gateway to the past and a springboard for a fuller understanding of Salamanca's cultural legacy.

Address: Puento Romano, 37008 Salamanca, spain.

Timings: 12.00am-11.59pm

Nearby hotel:

Hotel Ele Puente Roman de Salamanca

The location is just 3minutes walk to Roman Bridge and old Salamanca's old town. It has free parking on the street or the gas station at the front of the hotel. The rooms are big, clean comfortable and the Staff are helpful. Good breakfast buffet with fresh food of variety of options.

To the city centre: 1.7km

Nearest Airport: Salamanca Matacan

Distance to airport: 14.3km

Check-in time: 14.00

Check-out time: 12.00

Cost price: It vary depending on when you plan to stay and what room type you require. The average nightly room price has been $82

The Salamanca Rana

The University of Salamanca's elaborate façade conceals La Rana de Salamanca, or the Frog of Salamanca, a singular and intriguing tourist destination. For ages, this seemingly insignificant yet important element has piqued tourists' attention and enticed them to discover its secrets and the deeper significance of its presence.

What to see:

- Be on the lookout for La Rana, a secret treasure at Salamanca University. It is subtly placed on the building's exterior, among the numerous carvings and artistic accents. If you look attentively, you may see the frog hiding inside the elaborate masonry.

- The frog itself is a deftly carved figure that has been produced with amazing attention to detail and accuracy. Even though it is little, the aura of mystery that surrounds it and its enigmatic presence capture the mind.

Things to do:
- La Rana de Salamanca requires interaction that goes beyond simple observation. You can do the following things to improve your experience:

Locate the frog:
- Try to locate La Rana amidst the University's façade's numerous decorations. Make it into a fun game of discovery where the anticipation grows with every sighting of the frog.

To take a picture:
- Once you've located La Rana, take a picture to remember the occasion. It acts as a concrete reminder of your trip and the intriguing symbolism connected with this well-kept secret.

Think about what it means:

- Learn more about La Rana de Salamanca's symbolism. Consider its relevance in light of the University's history and traditions as you investigate the folklore and stories that surround it.

Tips for touring:

- Keeping the following in mind will help you get the most out of your trip to La Rana de Salamanca:

Look into the symbolism:

- Investigate the myths and symbolism surrounding La Rana before going there. This background information will improve your comprehension and help you realize the complexity of this seemingly unimportant figure.

Be a part of a tour:

- Take into account signing up for a University of Salamanca trip. Expert tours can offer unique insights into the institution's history, architecture, and undiscovered gems, such as La Rana.

Be open-minded:

- Keep an open mind and appreciate the mystery and fascination that surround La Rana de Salamanca as you explore it. Allow your imagination to soar as you become engrossed in the tales and interpretations.

Insights:

Both locals and visitors retain a particular place in their hearts for La Rana de Salamanca. It is more than just a decorative element on the University of Salamanca's façade; it also represents protection, good fortune, and undiscovered wisdom.

The frog is the subject of several myths and legends, some of which claim that discovering it would lead to scholastic achievement or a bright future. Others assert that making a wish or caressing the frog's nose will bring good fortune.

La Rana represents Salamanca's rich cultural legacy and customs in addition to its folklore. It serves as a reminder of the skilled craftsmanship and meticulous attention to detail that are evident throughout the city's magnificent structures.

La Rana de Salamanca may seem unremarkable to the untrained eye, but it has importance that goes beyond its appearance. It is a representation of the University's history, a covert guardian keeping watch on the pursuit of knowledge inside its confines.

The opportunity to interact with Salamanca's magical side, learn about its legends, and embrace its long-standing customs is provided by a trip to La Rana de Salamanca. The wonder and mystery that pervade Salamanca's cultural tapestry are invited you to immerse yourself in.

Consider the centuries of knowledge and intellectual endeavour that have occurred within the University's walls as you stand in front of La Rana de Salamanca. Take into account all the students who have entered in search of wisdom and information. The frog serves as a metaphor for the transforming potential of education, serving as a reminder of the significant influence that education can have on both people and society.

La Rana also serves as a reminder that sometimes the most important discoveries are made right in front of us. It teaches us to focus on the small things and to explore our surroundings with curiosity and an open mind. La Rana asks you to take a moment to pause and notice the beauty and significance of the seemingly unimportant in a busy city full with magnificent architectural masterpieces.

La Rana de Salamanca's presence adds a level of mystery and enchantment to your exploration of the University, whether you see it as a lucky charm, a representation of academic success, or a reminder of Salamanca's artistic past. It serves as a reminder that there is always more to learn, both within and outside of the academic community.

So, when you go to Salamanca University, start looking for La Rana. Let your imagination soar and your curiosity be aroused by its concealed presence. Take a minute to enjoy the legends, symbolism, and rich heritage that this tiny frog embodies as you stand in its presence. Let it motivate you to explore Salamanca's mysteries further and to come to terms with the mysticism that resides within its ancient walls.

La Rana de Salamanca is a charming fusion of mythology, history, and architectural beauty—a real jewel just waiting to be found by those who are eager to look for it. Let it serve as a reminder to investigate Salamanca, to think critically, and to enjoy its hidden gems as a sign of your journey.

Address: Calle Libreros, 19, 37008 Salamanca, Spain
Timings: Open 24 hours everyday
Phone: +34923294400

Map of Salamanca Rana

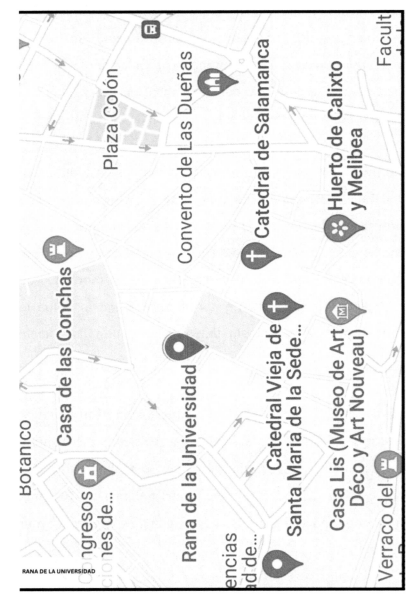

CHAPTER 4

Accommodation Options

Finding the ideal lodging is an important part of organizing any vacation, and Salamanca provides a wide variety of options to accommodate any traveler's requirements and interests. Salamanca has a range of lodging options to suit all tastes and budgets, including opulent hotels, comfortable guesthouses, and affordable hostels.

Salamanca has something to offer everyone, whether you're looking for a convenient location close to the major attractions or a peaceful getaway away from the busy city center. The lodging in Salamanca will make sure you have a pleasant and enjoyable stay throughout your visit to this magical city thanks to its attractive architecture, gracious hospitality, and practical conveniences.

Map of NH Hotel

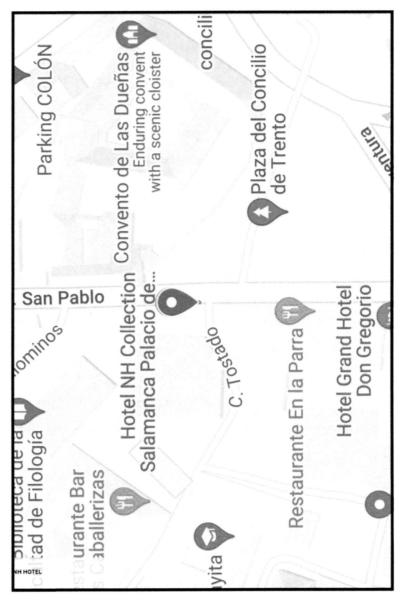

Map of Eurostars las claras

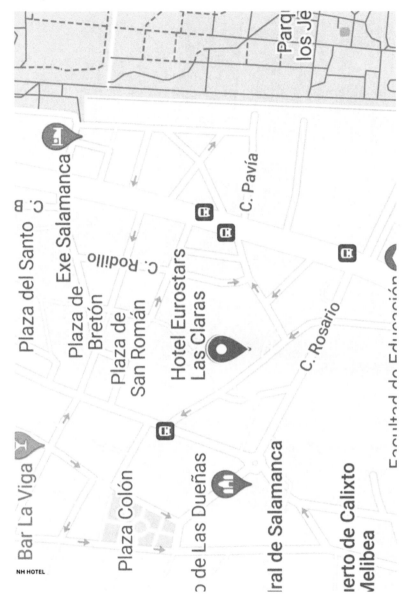

Hotel

The Salamanca hotel

Price: Nightly rates begin at $150.

Address: Salamanca, Spain, Calle de Teso de la Feria 2, 37008.

The check-in and check-out times: 2:00 PM and 12:00 PM, respectively.

Amenities:

The Parador de Salamanca has a restaurant serving traditional Spanish fare, a bar/lounge area, free Wi-Fi, a fitness facility, and breathtaking views of the city. The hotel's rooms are roomy and well appointed. The hotel also offers visitors easy access to on-site parking.

Abba Fonseca Hotel

Price: Nightly rates start at $100.

Location: Plaza San Blas, 2-4, Salamanca, Spain, 37007.

Phone: +34923011010

Email: fonseca@abbahotels.com

Check-In and Check-Out Times: Check-in is from 3:00 PM to 12:00 PM and vice versa.

Amenities

The Hotel Abba Fonseca offers a variety of amenities, including chic and cheerful rooms, a restaurant on-site serving a variety of regional and foreign cuisines, a comfortable lounge area, free WiFi, a 24-hour front desk, and a terrace with sweeping views of Salamanca's skyline. The hotel is also conveniently placed close to a number of tourist hotspots and transportation hubs.

NH Puerta de la Catedral in Salamanca

Price: Nightly rates begin at $80.

Address: Salamanca, Spain, Plaza Juan XXIII, 5, 37008.

Distance: 0.94km from Salamanca city centre and 13.89km from Salamanca airport

Check-In and Check-Out Times: Check-in is from 3:00 PM to 12:00 PM and vice versa.

Amenities:

Modern and trendy accommodations, a restaurant providing regional and international fare, a bar/lounge area, free WiFi, a fitness center, and a business center are all provided by NH Salamanca Puerta de la Catedral. Salamanca's key attractions, including as the Cathedral and Plaza Mayor, are conveniently accessible from the hotel thanks to its excellent position.

Inn Rector

Price: Nightly rates begin at $120.

Address: Salamanca, Spain, Paseo Rector Esperabe 10, 37008.

Phone: +34923218482

The check-in and check-out times: 2:00 PM and 12:00 PM, respectively.

Amenities:

The attractive and uniquely furnished rooms at Hotel Rector come with a garden terrace, a library, free WiFi, a bar, and a comfortable sitting area. The hotel's tranquil setting offers a tranquil escape from the busy city while still being close to the major attractions.

Vincci Salamanca City

Price: Nightly rates begin at $70.

Address: 26–28 Avenida de los Padres Paules, Salamanca, Spain, 37008.

The check-in and check-out times: 2:00 PM and 12:00 PM, respectively.

Vincci Ciudad de Salamanca features a restaurant with a variety of delectable dishes, a bar/lounge area, free Wi-Fi, a fitness center, and private parking. The hotel's advantageous position makes it simple to reach Salamanca's tourist sites and retail areas.

Take into account your spending limit, ideal location, and desired amenities while selecting a hotel in Salamanca. These alternatives offer a variety of possibilities to fit various preferences and guarantee a pleasurable stay in this historic city.

Price varies depending on the season and type of room required.

Hostel

Budget-Friendly Hostels in Salamanca: Liven Up Your Backpacking Experience

Residence Mindanao

Price: Nightly rates start at $20.

Address: 17 Avenida Italia, Salamanca, Spain, 37007.

The check-in and check-out times: 2:00 PM and 12:00 PM, respectively.

Amenities:

Hostal Mindanao provides inexpensive dormitory-style rooms with shared bathrooms, free WiFi, a guest-use kitchen, a comfortable lounge area, and a knowledgeable staff that may offer recommendations and help about the area.

The Concejo Hotel

Price: Nightly rates start at $25.

Address: Salamanca, Spain, Plaza de la Libertad 1, 37002.

Check-In and Check-Out Times: Check-in is from 3:00 PM to 12:00 PM and vice versa.

Amenities:

For the convenience of its visitors, Hostal Concejo offers reasonably priced private and shared rooms, communal bathrooms, free WiFi, a common area for gathering, luggage storage options, and a round-the-clock front desk.

Hostal Reise

Price: Nightly rates begin at $30.

Address: Salamanca, Spain, Calle Azafranal 14, 37001.

The check-in and check-out times: 2:00 PM and 12:00 PM, respectively.

Amenities:

Budget-friendly private and shared rooms, shared bathrooms, free Wi-Fi, a common area lounge, a vending machine for snacks and beverages, and a prime location close to the city center and major attractions are all provided by Hostal Reise.

Plaza Mayor Hotel

Price: Nightly rates start at $35.

Address: Plaza del Corrillo, 20. Salamanca, Spain 37002.
The check-in and check-out times: 2:00 PM and 12:00 PM, respectively.

Hostal Plaza Mayor's amenities include inexpensive private and shared rooms, shared bathrooms, free WiFi, a guest-use kitchen, a 24-hour front desk, and a superb position just steps from the Plaza Mayor and other important sites.

Hostels in Salamanca are a great option for tourists on a tight budget who want to experience a lively community. These hostels offer inexpensive lodging alternatives, fundamental conveniences, and quick access to the city's top attractions. During your visit to Salamanca, get into the backpacker mindset, meet other travelers, and make lifelong experiences.

Guesthouses

Guesthouses in Salamanca That Are Warmly Welcomed:

Inn at Cuzco
Price: Nightly rates begin at $50.

Address: Salamanca, Spain, Calle Pozo Amarillo 18, 37002.

The check-in and check-out times: 2:00 PM and 12:00 PM, respectively.

Amenities:

The comfortable and reasonably priced Hostal Cuzco offers individual rooms with en-suite bathrooms, free Wi-Fi, air conditioning, and heating, as well as a 24-hour front desk and a welcoming common area where visitors can unwind and mingle.

Los Infantes Hostal

Distance: 0.8 miles from centre of Salamanca and 7.8 miles to Salamanca matacan airport.

Price: Nightly rates begin at $60.

Address: Paseo De La Estacion, 125, 37006 Salamanca, Spain.

Check-In and Check-Out Times: Check-in is from 3:00 PM to 12:00 PM and vice versa.

Amenities:

The welcoming staff at Hostal Los Infantes is available to help with any needs, and the hotel offers comfortable, well-equipped rooms with private bathrooms, free Wi-Fi, air conditioning, heating, a terrace, and luggage storage.

Santel San Marcos Hotel

Price: Nightly rates begin at $80.

Address: Plaza San Marcos 7, Salamanca, Spain, 37002.

Phone: +34923269523

Check-In and Check-Out Times: Check-in is from 3:00 PM to 12:00 PM and vice versa.

Amenities:

The pleasant and well-appointed rooms of Hostal Santel San Marcos include private bathrooms, free Wi-Fi, air conditioning, heating, a 24-hour front desk, baggage storage, and a convenient location close to the Plaza Mayor and other famous sites.

Plaza Mayor Hotel

Price: Nightly rates begin at $90.

Address: Plaza Mayor, 24 in Salamanca, Spain, 37002.

The check-in and check-out times: 2:00 PM and 12:00 PM, respectively.

Amenities

With private bathrooms, free Wi-Fi, air conditioning, heating, a communal lounge area, a patio, and a prime position with views of the famous Plaza Mayor, Hostal Plaza Mayor offers guests pleasant and roomy accommodations.

To feel the warmth of Salamancan hospitality, choose a hostel. These lodgings provide reasonable pricing, nice rooms, and a variety of services to guarantee a relaxing and delightful stay in this fascinating city. During your stay to Salamanca, immerse yourself in the culture, uncover hidden jewels, and make enduring memories.

Apartments

Apartamentos Ra Mayor

Price: Nightly rates start at $100.

Address: 6, Calle Rá Mayor, Salamanca, Spain, 37002.

Check-In and Check-Out Times: Check-in is from 3:00 PM to 12:00 PM and vice versa.

Amenities:

Apartments at Apartamentos Ra Mayor are fully furnished, come with fully functional kitchens, private bathrooms, free Wi-Fi, air conditioning, and heating, and are conveniently located close to the Plaza Mayor and other points of interest.

Residences JCH Congreso

Price: Nightly rates begin at $150.

Address: Salamanca, Spain, Calle Azafranal 18, 37001.

Check-In and Check-Out Times: Check-in is from 3:00 PM to 12:00 PM and vice versa.

Amenities:

The cozy and luxurious apartments at Apartamentos JCH Congreso include completely furnished kitchens, private bathrooms, free Wi-Fi, air conditioning, heating, a lounge area, and a convenient position close to the city's core and important attractions.

Apartments Toro 33
Price: Nightly rates begin at $180.
Address: Calle Toro, 33, Salamanca, Spain, 37002.
The check-in and check-out times: 2:00 PM and 12:00 PM, respectively.

Amenities:
Modern, roomy apartments with living areas, fully functional kitchens, private bathrooms, free Wi-Fi, air conditioning, and heating are available at Apartamentos Toro 33, which is also conveniently located near the Plaza Mayor and other well-known attractions.

When visiting Salamanca, take advantage of the independence and convenience of living in an apartment. These lodgings give you the option to make your own meals at home and offer a variety of facilities and roomy living spaces. During your visit to Salamanca, immerse yourself in the culture, see the city at your own speed, and create lifelong memories.

CHAPTER 5

The cuisine of Salamanca

G et ready to go out on a gastronomic voyage packed with tantalizing flavors, enticing fragrances, and scrumptious delicacies that will leave you wanting more. Salamanca's culinary culture is steeped in tradition and is influenced by the bounty of regional delicacies and time-tested traditions that have been handed down through the years.

The city's numerous food selections, which range from delicious meats and cheeses to fresh seafood and seasonal veggies, reflect the area's agricultural abundance and culinary skill. Discovering the local markets, like Mercado Central, can help you get started on your culinary journey. Here, you can immerse yourself in a colorful environment that is buzzing with the colors and fragrances of fresh fruits, vegetables, meats, and artisanal goods.

Meet welcoming sellers, gain knowledge of local delicacies, and find out about the distinctive ingredients that characterize Salamanca's cuisine.

The cured ham created from Iberian pigs reared on acorns is known as jamón ibérico, and no trip to Salamanca would be complete without tasting it. Enjoy this delicacy's delicate texture and robust flavor for a minute as you consider why it is regarded as one of Spain's culinary gems.

Salamanca's local cuisine

Salamanca is a treasure mine of flavors and gastronomic pleasures when it comes to traditional food. Take a culinary tour of the city's diverse cuisine to learn about the traditional meals that have endured the test of time and continue to entice diners from all over the world.

Visit these renowned eateries that highlight the best of regional cuisines to thoroughly experience Salamanca's traditional cuisine:

1. Cervantes, Mesón

Traditional Castilian food is the centerpiece of Mesón Cervantes, which specializes in robust meat dishes like roasted lamb and tender beef. Additionally, they provide a wide selection of delectable tapas that go excellently with their comprehensive wine list.

Cost: Depending on the options, prices per person range from $20 to $40.

Address: Salamanca, Spain, Plaza San Boal 2, 37002.

2. El Mesón de Gonzalo Restaurant

Spanish cuisine at El Mesón de Gonzalo is renowned for being superb and showcasing regional flavors. Enjoy foods like iberico ham, Castilian soups, and succulent grilled meats. For a genuine sense of Salamanca, their menu also includes seasonal delicacies.

Cost: Prices range, with a $30 to $50 per person average.

Address: Salamanca, Spain, Calle Bordadores 5, 37002.

3. Don Mauro's Restaurant

The cuisine at Don Mauro combine traditional and cutting-edge cooking techniques while presenting the finest regional ingredients. Their menu honors the tastes of Salamanca with dishes like grilled Iberian pork and creamy salmorejo (cold tomato soup).

Cost: Prices per person range from $25 to $45.

Address: Salamanca, Spain, Calle Iscar Peyra 10, 37008.

4. The Victor Gutiérrez Restaurant

Victor Gutiérrez offers a chic and modern interpretation of classical food. Their Michelin-starred meal offers a distinctive culinary experience by fusing contemporary methods with age-old ingredients.

Cost: The tasting menu's prices start at $80 per person.

Address: Calle Paseo de la Estación, 32, Salamanca, Spain (37004).

Visit these renowned eateries to tantalize your palate and savor the tastes of Salamanca's regional cuisine. Each mouthful will convey you to the heart of the city's culinary legacy, from tender meats to mouthwatering tapas. Enjoy the chance to indulge in regional dishes while sipping on area wines for a memorable dining experience in Salamanca.

Food and Drinks You Must Try

La Viga Bar

The starting price for each dish is $10.

A quaint and well-liked location, Bar La Viga is well-known for its delectable seafood dishes. Enjoy their delicious prawns, mouthwatering grilled octopus, and fresh fish tapas. For a delicious dining experience, sip a cool glass of local white wine with your meal.

Location: Spain, Salamanca, Calle de los Serranos 11, 37008.

El Corrillo Mesón

The starting price for each dish is $15.

Offering a variety of traditional Spanish meals with a contemporary twist is Mesón El Corrillo. Don't pass up their tasty roasted lamb, creamy paella, and succulent Iberian pork cheeks. For a supper that is truly gratifying, serve a glass of powerful red wine with it.

Address: Plaza Mayor, 19, Salamanca, Spain, 37002.

Casa Paca Restaurant

The starting price for each dish is $20.

The restaurant Casa Paca is well known for serving traditional Spanish fare. Try their tender suckling pig, flavorful Iberian ham croquettes, and succulent octopus prepared in Galician style. To complete your culinary trip, serve a pitcher of chilled sangria with your dinner.

Address: Salamanca, Spain, Calle Quintana 10, 37002.

El Oso and the Madro

The starting price for a drink is $8.

A variety of specialty beers and Spanish wines are available in the bustling tavern El Oso y el Madroo. Enjoy a glass of Rioja, sample a crisp Albario, or discover the range of regional specialty beers. This bar is ideal for spending an enjoyable evening with friends because of its lively environment and welcoming staff.

Address: Salamanca, Spain, Plaza de San Juan Bautista, 5, 37002.

Monterrey Bar

The starting price for a drink is $5.

The well-liked neighborhood bar Bar Monterrey is well-known for its energizing concoctions. Try one of their famous Mojitos, indulge in a traditional Gin & Tonic, or sip on a tropical Pia Colada. The bar's vibrant atmosphere and talented mixologists make it a fantastic place to unwind and savor a tasty beverage.

Salamanca's gastronomic gems will tantalize your palate. These places provide a variety of tastes and experiences, including luscious meats, delicious seafood, fine wines, and refreshing cocktails. With each nibble and drink, discover Salamanca's culinary delights and make lifelong memories.

Neighborhood Cafés and Restaurants

Novelty Café

The starting price for each dish is $10.

In the center of Salamanca, there is a classic café called Café Novelty. Enjoy their exquisite pastries, tasty sandwiches, and delectable tapas. Enjoy a cup of creamy coffee while you take in the pleasant atmosphere of the café and the views of Plaza Mayor.

Address: Salamanca, Spain, Plaza Mayor 1, 37002.

El Mesón de Gonzalo Restaurant

The starting price for each dish is $25.

A renowned restaurant, Restaurante El Meson de Gonzalo offers classic Spanish fare with a modern twist. Taste their mouthwatering roasted meats, crisp fish, and decadent desserts. The welcoming environment enhances the overall dining experience.

Address: Salamanca, Spain, Calle de Bordadores 5, 37002.

Inna Taberna

The starting price for each dish is $15.

A cozy restaurant serving local Salamanca food is called Taberna Charra. Enjoy their famous suckling pig roast, savory stews, and regional cured meats. As you enjoy your meal and the rustic appeal of this quaint restaurant, pair it with a glass of superb Spanish wine.

Don Mauro's Restaurant

The starting price for each dish is $20.

Mediterranean and cosmopolitan cuisines are combined at the restaurant Don Mauro. Enjoy their imaginative food, which is prepared using local, fresh ingredients. This restaurant offers a distinctive and enjoyable dining experience, featuring luscious grilled meats and delicate seafood specialties.

Madrid's Café Bar Restaurant

The starting price for each dish is $12.

Madrid's Café Bar Restaurante is a well-liked hangout for both locals and tourists. Take advantage of their large menu, which includes traditional Spanish fare like paella, tapas, and grilled meats. For a great eating experience, sip a crisp lager or a beautiful glass of Spanish wine with your meal.

Address: Salamanca, Spain, Calle Iscar Peyra 2, 37002.

Explore these neighborhood eateries and restaurants as you embark on a culinary tour in Salamanca. These places provide a wide variety of tastes and sensations, from traditional Spanish cuisine to cutting-edge culinary inventions. Enjoy every bite of Salamanca's diverse cuisine as you travel across the city.

CHAPTER 6

Shopping in Salamanca

Welcome to Salamanca's bustling commercial district!, this ancient city provides a fascinating combination of conventional charm and contemporary shopping opportunities. Salamanca offers everything a shopper might want in terms of shopping, from crowded marketplaces to stylish boutiques and department stores.

Salamanca offers a shopping experience that combines style, tradition, and the warmth of Spanish hospitality, whether you're looking for the newest fashion trends, regional specialties, or one-of-a-kind souvenirs. Prepare to go on a shopping adventure and find the hidden gems Salamanca's lovely streets have to offer.

Popular Shopping

El Corte Ingles

Opening Times: Monday through Saturday, 10:00 AM to 10:00 PM; closed on Sunday.

El Corte Inglés is a well-known department store that sells a variety of goods, such as clothing, accessories, cosmetics, home goods, and technology. Enjoy a great shopping experience as you explore numerous floors loaded with both Spanish and international brands.

Calle Toro

Opening Times: These vary each store, but are typically 10:00 AM to 9:00 PM.

Address: Calle Toro, Salamanca, Spain, 37002.

A variety of shops, boutiques, and speciality businesses along the bustling shopping strip known as Calle Toro. Learn about clothing businesses, jewelry stores, and more. Wander around casually and look into the various store possibilities.

El Tormes Commercial Center

Opening Times: Monday through Saturday, 10:00 AM to 10:00 PM; closed on Sunday.

Location: Calle del Rio Tormes, s/n, Salamanca, Spain, 37008.

Modern shopping complex Centro Comercial El Tormes houses a variety of domestic and foreign brands. You may find a wide range of things to meet your needs, from clothing and accessories to electronics and home design. Convenient and fun shopping is available under one roof.

Salamanca Central Market

Opening Times: 8:00 AM to 2:30 PM, Monday through Saturday.

Address: Salamanca, Spain 37001, Plaza del Mercado.

Fresh fruit, meats, cheeses, baked goods, and other items may be found at the lively Mercado Central de Salamanca. Experience Salamanca's genuine flavors while interacting with neighborhood merchants and soaking up the lively ambiance.

The Gallery

Opening Times: 10:30 AM - 2:00 PM, 5:30 PM - 8:30 PM, Monday through Friday; 10:30 AM - 2:00 PM, Saturday.

Address: 14 Calle Quintana, Salamanca, Spain, 37002.

La Galera is a beautiful shop that offers a carefully curated collection of one-of-a-kind and handcrafted goods. Learn about handcrafted jewelry, accessories, furniture, and artwork. Find one-of-a-kind items to bring home as keepsakes while supporting regional artists.

Discover Salamanca's shopping district and have a fantastic shopping experience. These shopping locations offer a wide variety of options to suit your interests and preferences, whether you're seeking for fashion, regional specialties, or one-of-a-kind items. Navigate the city's shopping streets an centers and savor the rush of discovering something unique.

Regional Markets

Salamanca Central Market

Opening Times: 8:00 AM to 2:30 PM, Monday through Saturday.

Address: Salamanca, Spain 37001, Plaza del Mercado.

The top local products, meats, cheeses, and more are on display at the Mercado Central de Salamanca, a bustling market. This vibrant market, which is open every day of the week, welcomes you to take part in the lively environment, interact with the welcoming merchants, and experience the genuine tastes of Salamanca.

The market offers a wide variety of things for both locals and tourists to enjoy, ranging from fresh fruits and vegetables to mouthwatering baked goods and regional specialties.

Market of San Juan

Opening Times: Monday through Friday, 5:00 PM to 8:00 PM; Saturday, 9:30 AM to 2:30 PM.

A lovely market recognized for its assortment of premium culinary items, Mercado de San Juan is situated close to the

San Juan Bautista Church. Fresh fruits, vegetables, meats, seafood, and gourmet treats are all available here. Investigate the stalls, strike up a dialog with the exhibitors, and learn about the components of Salamanca's thriving food scene.

Salamanca's Abastos Market

Opening Times: 8:00 AM to 2:30 PM, Monday through Saturday.

Locals assemble at the historic Mercado de Abastos de Salamanca to buy the ingredients for their daily meals. The market offers a wide variety of commodities, from farm-fresh fruit to handcrafted crafts. Explore the booths that are packed with stalls of local cheeses, beautiful fruits, and spices. Take in the lively ambiance, savor the genuine flavors, and discover the true essence of Salamanca's cuisine.

The La Alamedilla Market

Opening Times: Monday through Friday, 5:00 pm to 8:00 pm; Saturday, 8:00 am to 3:00 pm.

Address: Plaza de Barcelona, Salamanca, Spain, 37007.

The Alamedilla neighborhood's Mercado de La Alamedilla provides a wide range of fresh goods that are sourced directly from regional farmers. Investigate the market's stalls, which are stocked with seasonal meats, veggies, and other foods. The market offers a wide range of gastronomic options, from local specialties to foreign products. Engage in conversation with the welcoming merchants, collect materials for a homemade meal, or just take in the lively ambience of this neighborhood meeting spot.

Don't pass up the chance to visit these lively neighborhood markets while you are in Salamanca. They offer an immersive experience where you may enjoy your senses, learn about the culinary gems of the area, and interact with the welcoming sellers that bring Salamanca's delicacies to life.

These markets provide a fascinating tour into the center of Salamanca's culinary scene, whether you're looking for fresh ingredients for a home-cooked meal or simply want to immerse yourself in the local culture.

Souvenirs and Unique Finds

Salamanca artisans

Opening Times: 10:00 AM to 8:00 PM, Monday through Saturday.

Address: Salamanca, Spain, Calle de Zamora 10, 37002.

In the center of the city, Artesana Salamanca is a beautiful store that sells a variety of handcrafted items and distinctive trinkets. This shop honors Salamanca's artistic past with gorgeous fabrics, jewelry, and intricately created ceramics. Explore their inventory to find one-of-a-kind items that perfectly express the craftsmanship and traditions of the neighborhood.

The Cathedral Store

Opening times: 10:00 AM to 8:00 PM, Monday through Sunday.

La Tienda de la Catedral, a charming store next to the cathedral, is stocked with religious relics, home accents, and mementos drawn from the city's famous cathedral. This shop offers a distinctive assortment of things that reflect the spiritual and cultural value of Salamanca, including small replicas of the cathedral, religious icons, and handcrafted ornaments.

Bookstore Casa de las Conchas

Opening Times: Monday through Friday, 5:00 pm to 8:00 pm; Saturday, 8:00 am to 2:00 pm.

Monday through Friday, 9:00 to 15:00 during the summer.

Address: Salamanca, Spain, Calle Compaa 2, 37002.

his bookstore, which is located inside the historic Casa de las Conchas, is a refuge for readers and history buffs. Peruse their library's selection of books, which includes volumes on the literature, art, and history of the region. Additionally, the store sells a variety of one-of-a-kind trinkets including postcards, tote bags, and bookmarks that feature the iconic shell design.

Market of Artists

Opening times: 11:00 AM to 9:00 PM on Saturdays and Sundays.

On the weekends, a bustling artisan market called Mercado de Artesana displays the work of regional artisans. Explore the booths filled with handcrafted jewelry, leather products, textiles, and other works of art. Engage with the craftspeople, discover their methods, and locate one-of-a-kind mementos that showcase the artistry and ability of Salamanca.

You may take a piece of Salamanca's culture and history home with you by perusing the city's gift shops and artisan boutiques. These shops provide a wide variety of one-of-a-kind finds that serve as treasured mementos of your time in Salamanca, from finely produced pottery to literary gems and religious objects. So take your time, go around the stores, and discover the ideal souvenir that embodies the charm of this captivating city.

CHAPTER 7

Events and Festivals in Salamanca

Salamanca is a city that comes alive with a variety of festivals and events throughout the year. It is noted for its rich cultural legacy and lively environment. The city offers a broad calendar of celebrations that enthrall both residents and visitors, from historic customs to modern celebrations of art and music. Join in the fun and embrace the distinctive cultural experiences that these festivals and events have to offer to fully experience Salamanca's vibrant community.The holy week (Semana Santa)

In Salamanca, a Season of Solemnity and Devotion

Date: Variable each year, typically occurring in March or April.

Time: Processions occur throughout the week at various hours of the day and night.

In Salamanca, Semana Santa, or Holy Week, is a greatly anticipated and treasured holiday. Every year during the spring, the city celebrates this week-long event, which is of great religious significance and serves as a moving reminder of the city's rich Catholic tradition.

The streets of Salamanca come to life during Semana Santa with a number of solemn processions that portray the last days of Jesus Christ's life, which culminated in his crucifixion and resurrection. Groups of committed people carrying elaborate floats called pasos along the twisting lanes while wearing traditional garb and listening to hauntingly beautiful music. These processions are an inspiring demonstration of faith and devotion that implores both participants and onlookers to consider the suffering and death of Christ.

During Semana Santa, there is a reverent and reflective mood. The streets are decorated with flower accents, and incense is wafting through the air. People assemble to watch the processions and show their respect for the deceased. Saetas, spontaneous devotional songs performed from rooftops and balconies, add to the seriousness of the event with their eerie sound.

Each procession during Semana Santa represents a particular scene from the biblical story and is unique to the day. These processions provide a visual picture of the pivotal moments in Christian religion, from Jesus' joyous entry into Jerusalem to the sorrowful mourning of his crucifixion.

The Santo Entierro (Holy Burial) march at night is one of Semana Santa's most recognizable and stirring events. This mournful procession is held on Good Friday and features black-draped pasos being carried silently through the streets while being occasionally interrupted by church bells tolling. A sense of collective sadness and reflection is evoked by this extraordinarily powerful encounter.

Locals and visitors to Salamanca can experience a deeply ingrained tradition and make a spiritual connection during Semana Santa. The experience is sure to make a lasting memory, whether you take part in the processions or watch from the sidelines. It is a time to honor Salamanca's rich cultural and religious past and to reflect on the timeless ideas of faith, giving one's all, and atonement.

Check the precise dates of Semana Santa as you prepare for your trip to Salamanca because they can change from year to year. Semana Santa is a very spiritual experience, so immerse yourself in it by embracing the solemnity and devotion that permeate the city throughout this holy week.

Castilla y León International Festival of the Arts

Salamanca Celebrates Art and Creativity

Date: Every year varies; usually takes place in the summer.

Time: Events and performances are scheduled at various times throughout the festival, both during the day and at night.

A widely anticipated cultural occasion, the Festival Internacional de las Artes de Castilla y León (FACYL) brings together artists from diverse fields to display their skills in Salamanca, a beautiful city. This exciting event honors art, creativity, and the power of human expression and is held every year in the summer.

In order to offer a genuinely immersive experience, FACYL converts the city into a mesmerizing stage where theater, dance, music, visual arts, and other artistic disciplines converge. The exhibition of the works of local and international artists creates a diversified and dynamic environment that incorporates both traditional and contemporary art forms.

The festival provides a wide range of possibilities for both artists and spectators to connect with the arts through its varied program of performances, exhibitions, seminars, and interactive installations. Each event at FACYL aspires to engage, inspire, and challenge the senses, from thought-provoking theatre presentations to breathtaking dance performances.

The dedication of FACYL to promoting both well-known musicians and up-and-coming artists is one of its distinctive features. Young performers, musicians, and visual artists can use this as a platform to get noticed and express their artistic vision with a larger audience. It's a kaleidoscope of artistic expression that promotes creativity and calls for the discovery of new artistic terrain.

Salamanca is home to a number of locations where the festival is held, including cultural institutions, outdoor stages, and ancient theaters. These many locations enrich the entire experience by enabling visitors to take in the art world while learning about other aspects of the city.

FACYL includes conversations, seminars, and educational events that explore the creative process and provide insights into the art world in addition to the performances and exhibitions. It provides an opportunity for creatives and art lovers to interact, work together, and get inspired by one another.

Check the festival's itinerary as you prepare to visit Salamanca to make sure your trip coincides with FACYL's dates. This festival presents a fantastic opportunity to immerse yourself in the world of art, experience the transformational force of artistic expression, and appreciate the various manifestations of human creativity, whether you're an enthusiastic art lover or simply curious about the creative spirit.

As artists from all over the world congregate in Salamanca to share their experiences, opinions, and creative visions, get ready to be captivated by the sheer talent and creativity on exhibit. FACYL is a tribute to the continuing influence of art and to how it can bridge cultural divides, spark debate, and uplift us all.

A Festive Celebration of Tradition and Fun in Salamanca

Date: Every year varies; usually occurs around September.

Time: Events and activities are scheduled throughout the duration of the festival at various hours during the day and at night.

The Feria de Salamanca is a colorful and energetic event that takes place in Salamanca, a charming city that offers a joyous celebration of regional customs, music, dance, and cuisine. This festival, which takes place every September, is a well-liked occasion that draws both locals and tourists, fostering a joyful atmosphere that celebrates Salamanca's rich cultural legacy.

The city comes to life with a kaleidoscope of hues, noises, and flavors during the Feria de Salamanca. A magnificent opening ceremony that features parades, traditional dances, and live music sets the celebration beginning. The city immediately changes into a center of excitement, offering a wide variety of activities for people of all ages and interests.

The lively fairground, where amusement rides, games, and attractions produce an exhilarating atmosphere, is one of the highlights of the Feria de Salamanca. Take a stroll through the lively streets packed with booths and stands that are selling a range of crafts, regional goods, and mouthwatering foods. You can experience Salamancan cuisine, engage with local artisans, and fully immerse oneself in the culture of the region.

The festival's rhythmic and melodic performances of traditional music and dance fill the air. You'll have the chance to see mesmerizing performances that highlight the area's rich musical legacy, from flamenco to folk music. Join in the dancing, pick up a few moves, and let the beat direct your steps.

The Feria de Salamanca also hosts cultural exhibitions, workshops, and performances that provide a window into the customs and crafts of the region. These cultural experiences provide tourists a deeper insight of Salamanca's cultural heritage and give them the chance to interact with the local population, whether it be through a demonstration of traditional pottery manufacturing or a display of traditional costumes.

The Feria de Salamanca has a strong emphasis on food, offering a wide variety of culinary pleasures to suit every taste. Taste regional specialties like Jamón Ibérico, chorizo, and other tapas while taking in the festival's vibrant ambiance. Salamanca is famed for its great vineyards and wineries, so don't pass up the chance to indulge in some regional wines and spirits.

The Feria de Salamanca is an occasion to celebrate life, get lost in the vivid culture, and make enduring memories. To enjoy the fervor and delight of this cherished event, be sure to check the festival's schedule when you make travel arrangements to Salamanca. The Feria de Salamanca guarantees a joyful and unforgettable experience for everyone, whether you're dancing to the beat of traditional music, taking in the exhilarating carnival attractions, or savoring the delectable delicacies of Salamanca.

Festival of Corpus Christi

Salamanca's Spectacular Display of Faith and Tradition

Date: Each year is different, but it is usually in June.

Time: Throughout the day, with the morning being the time of the biggest parade.

During the Corpus Christi Festival, Salamanca comes to life with vivacious hues, rhythmic music, and a deep sense of devotion. This religious celebration, which takes place every June, is a noteworthy feature on the city's calendar and draws both residents and tourists to witness an amazing display of faith, creativity, and cultural heritage.

Salamanca's Corpus Christi Festival is well known for its elaborate procession through the city's cobblestone streets. This magnificent festival has grandiose religious floats portraying biblical events and saints that are covered with delicate floral decorations. Following the clergy, who are all dressed to the nines, are members of religious brotherhoods, local dignitaries, and the faithful.

A special Mass is usually held at the Cathedral to commemorate the Eucharist and to provide an opportunity for prayer at the start of the festival. Following the Mass, the procession begins, and the streets are covered in carpets of vibrant flower petals, producing a breathtaking sight. As the procession moves along the predetermined route, the rhythmic sound of traditional music fills the air, joined by the participants' solemn chants and prayers.

The careful artistry demonstrated in the construction of the religious floats is one of the centerpieces of the Corpus Christi Festival. Using a combination of carpentry, metalwork, and floral arrangements, these magnificent buildings are painstakingly made by expert craftspeople. Each float conveys a story from a religious text, allowing viewers to interact with the narratives and consider their own religious beliefs.

You will be engaged in a sensory experience unlike any other as you follow the procession. The scent of incense fills the room, contributing to the reverent and spiritual ambiance. Both residents and tourists throng the streets, anxious to see the procession and show their admiration for this ages-old custom.

It's crucial to remember that the Corpus Christi Festival has a strong religious foundation. As a result, it is advised that you dress appropriately and appreciate the occasion's solemnity. Respect the traditions and customs of your community and adhere to the guidance given by the clergy and event organizers.

The Salamanca Corpus Christi Festival features a variety of other activities and festivities throughout the day in addition to the main procession. You can tour the crowded markets and fairgrounds, where you can discover vibrant performances to enjoy, excellent food stalls providing regional specialties, and local craftsmen selling their wares.

Experiencing Salamanca's Corpus Christi Festival offers a singular chance to see how faith, art, and culture interact with one another. It is a moment when the entire city comes together to honor religious convictions and pay respect to long-standing customs that have helped Salamanca develop its unique identity. Take a moment to admire the beauty and profound meaning of this amazing display of devotion while you partake in the celebrations.

Verify the precise dates and hours of the activities if you intend to visit Salamanca during the Corpus Christi Festival by looking them up on the local calendar. Join the processions, embrace the festival's energy, and allow yourself to be mesmerized by the deeply ingrained customs and sincere religious emotions that make this celebration so extraordinary.

CHAPTER 8

Day Trips from Salamanca

If you want to broaden your perspective and travel outside of the city, you're in for a treat. The ideal starting place for amazing day trips to adjacent locations that each have their own special charms is Salamanca. There is something for every traveler's preference, from charming towns to natural treasures.

Ávila

Set your sights on the picturesque town of Vila, which is nearby if you're looking for an exciting day trip from Salamanca. Prepare to be transported back in time to the medieval age as you begin this expedition, where you will see imposing walls, historic cathedrals, and cobblestone alleys.

About 110 kilometers separate Salamanca from Vila, providing a wonderful trip through the lovely Spanish countryside. If you want convenience, think about hiring a car. Alternatively, choose a hassle-free mode of transportation like a bus or train to get where you're going.

Be ready to be astounded by Vila's immaculately preserved medieval walls when you first arrive. These remarkable defenses, which span nearly 2.5 kilometers, date back to the 11th century. Enjoy the expansive views of the town and the surroundings as you stroll leisurely around the walls. It's a fascinating experience that gives you a sense of the town's significant strategic role throughout history.

Visit the magnificent Vila Cathedral, a magnificent example of Gothic and Romanesque architecture, while you are in Vila. Enter and be amazed by the interior's meticulous decorations, which are enhanced by lovely stained-glass windows and elaborate altars. Spend a minute soaking up the tranquil atmosphere and appreciating how the generations of devotion have sculpted this holy place.

The Basilica de San Vicente is a magnificent Romanesque church that serves as a reminder of Vila's rich religious history. Admire the magnificent stone carvings on the façade before entering to see the interior's peaceful beauty.

You will come across gorgeous plazas, tiny shops, and classic Spanish homes as you stroll around Vila's charming streets. Enjoy a leisurely stroll through the lively town while stopping to sample regional specialties or look for keepsakes to remember your trip.

The price of the day trip will vary depending on the form of transportation you select and any other costs like meals or attraction admission fees. Budget appropriately and take into account any pre-booking possibilities to make your visit more convenient.

Vila awaits with its amazing history and appeal of the Middle Ages. Plan your day trip carefully, leaving enough time to see the town's top attractions and experience its distinctive atmosphere. As you travel back in time and uncover the mysteries of this medieval gem, Vila promises a day of exploration and magic, from the beautiful walls to the historic churches and the picturesque streets.

Segovia

A day excursion to the charming city of Segovia is essential if you want to explore Spain's incredible heritage beyond Salamanca's borders. This tour promises stunning scenery and a richness of cultural riches and is around 120 kilometers from Salamanca.

You can choose from a number of transportation options, such as buses or trains, to get to Segovia from Salamanca. The price of the journey will vary depending on your mode of transportation and any extra costs you may have along the way. To get the most out of your visit, it's a good idea to budget and plan appropriately.

Get ready to be mesmerized by Segovia's majestic sights as soon as you reach there. The city is well renowned for its famous Roman aqueduct, an early first-century engineering wonder. Admire the accuracy and magnificence of this historic building, which spans almost 800 meters and serves as a reminder of the Roman Empire's brilliance.

The Alcázar, a castle that looks like it belongs in a fantasy, is another must-see sight in Segovia. Wander around the different rooms and chambers, each with its own distinctive architectural design and ornamental features, to learn more about its rich past. The Alcázar provides a window into the city's regal past, from the towering Tower of John II to the breathtaking Throne Room.

Without taking in the splendor of the Segovia Cathedral, no trip to Segovia is complete. Admire the magnificent altarpiece, deftly crafted stained glass windows, and soaring Gothic architecture. Spend a minute taking in the spiritual atmosphere and admiring the skill that was used to create this masterpiece.

Segovia's streets are filled with quaint squares, scenic passageways, and undiscovered nooks just waiting to be explored. Indulge in a slice of Segovian cake or try the famed roasted suckling pig at one of the local eateries to get a taste of the food.

A fascinating fusion of history, architecture, and cultural immersion is promised by the day excursion from Salamanca to Segovia. Allow yourself to be carried away to a bygone period as you take your time to take in the grandeur of each monument. Take pictures of Segovia's charm or just stroll through the city's historic streets and take it all in.

Zamora

A day trip from Salamanca to Zamora is a great option if you're itching to discover the undiscovered jewels of the Castilla y León region. This trip, which is only about 90 kilometers away, will take you on an enthralling excursion through time and reveal the hidden gems of history and culture.

You can pick from a variety of transportation options, like buses or trains, to get from Salamanca to Zamora. Depending on your preferred method and any supplemental costs you may accrue while route, the cost of the trip will change. It's a good idea to budget appropriately to ensure a smooth and enjoyable visit.

Be prepared to be fascinated by Zamora's extensive historical legacy when you arrive. Wander through the winding alleyways and be enchanted by the various churches, castles, and fortified walls that highlight the city's medieval beauty. The city is recognized for its amazing collection of Romanesque architecture, earning it the moniker "The Romanesque City."

The magnificent Zamora Cathedral is among Zamora's features. Admire its magnificent architecture, which is distinguished by its particular Romanesque design. Step inside to see the interior's meticulous decorations, including the elaborate altars and beautiful stained glass windows that fill the room with a rainbow of hues.

Visit the Castle of Zamora, which is set on a hill above the city, as soon as you get the chance. Explore its historic walls and towers, which provide a window into Zamora's strategic past, while taking in the panoramic vistas. You can also take in breath-taking views of the surrounding surroundings from the castle.

Visit the Ethnographic Museum to discover more about the customs, crafts, and way of life that are unique to Zamora and its past. Learn about the area's rich history by becoming immersed in the local culture.

Spend some time indulging in the regional food while exploring Zamora. Enjoy traditional fare like roasted lamb, garlic soup, or the well-known tapas in the Zamora manner. Enjoy your dinner with a glass of the top wine produced in the area, which is renowned for its strong tastes and excellence.

A rich experience that blends history, architecture, and culinary delights is promised by the day excursion from Salamanca to Zamora. As you tour the city's outstanding landmarks and take in its lively atmosphere, allow yourself to be whisked back in time.

La Alberca

A day excursion from Salamanca to La Alberca is a great option if you're hoping to get away from the busy city and unwind in rural Spain. This charming community, which is around 75 kilometers away, welcomes you to explore its unspoiled beauty.

Consider the cost of transportation and any additional costs that might occur as you plan your day excursion. To ensure a smooth and comfortable voyage as you travel into the heart of La Alberca, it is important to set aside a budget.

You pass through picturesque terrain on the trip from Salamanca to La Alberca, with its rolling hills and lush green surroundings. You'll be enchanted by the village's enduring attractiveness and maintained traditional architecture as soon as you arrive.

Explore La Alberca's cobblestone streets and take in the preserved homes with stone facades and wooden balconies. Explore the Plaza Mayor, the village's central gathering place where you may take in the wonderful ambiance. This ancient square is surrounded by quaint stores, cafes, and eateries, making it the ideal place to unwind and take in the ambiance.

Visit the Church of Nuestra Seora de la Asunción to immerse yourself in the rich cultural legacy of La Alberca. Admire its exquisite interior, which includes ornate altarpieces and religious artwork that reflects the village's long-standing customs.

The surrounding natural beauty of La Alberca will enthrall nature lovers. Take a hike or a nature stroll to explore the picturesque surroundings of the village. With trails leading to beautiful overlooks and undiscovered waterfalls, the Sierra de Francia mountain range in the area provides breath-taking views and chances for outdoor experiences.

Enjoy regional cuisine by indulging in homey dishes at La Alberca's quaint eateries. Don't pass up the chance to sample the cured ham known as jamón ibérico, which is renowned for its excellent flavor. Allow yourself to enjoy the flavors of the place by serving your meal with a glass of local wine.

The day excursion to La Alberca from Salamanca promises a tranquil getaway to a lovely community tucked away in the embrace of nature. Let the tranquility of the surroundings and the kind welcome of the inhabitants take you back in time to a more carefree period so you may relax and take in the splendor of rural Spain.

La Alberca offers a tranquil getaway that will leave you feeling refreshed and inspired, regardless of whether you're looking for cultural immersion, beautiful scenery, or a break from the hustle and bustle of the city. Get ready to be mesmerized by this lovely village's rural charm and the surrounding natural wonders.

CHAPTER 9

Practical Information

I
t's crucial to have ready access to information that can help make your travel to Salamanca smooth and hassle-free when you set off on your adventure. These tips will guarantee a memorable trip in this bustling Spanish city, whether it be by assisting with navigating local traditions, transit, or the best restaurants.

You'll be well-prepared to navigate Salamanca with ease and enjoy your stay if you are familiar with these useful information.

Opening Times

- The majority of Salamanca's stores, eateries, and attractions adhere to the siesta schedule, which involves a brief afternoon closure. Businesses frequently close between 2:00 PM and 5:00 PM. Consider how you want to spend your time and keep in mind that certain businesses may have different hours on Sundays or on holidays.

Health and Safety Advice

Your wellbeing and safety should always come first when touring the fascinating city of Salamanca. You may have a worry-free and rewarding trip in this exciting Spanish location by heeding these health and safety recommendations.

Pay attention to your surroundings

- Salamanca is a fairly safe city, but you should always be on the lookout for potential dangers, especially in crowded places and popular tourist destinations. Keep an eye on your possessions and refrain from showing off expensive stuff too often.

Remain hydrated

- Salamanca has hot summers, so it's important to stay hydrated, especially if you're going outside. To avoid dehydration, keep a water bottle with you and consume a lot of fluids during the day. Public drinking fountains are another option where you can restock your bottle.

Defend yourself from the sun

- Particularly in the summer, the Spanish sun may be rather harsh. Before going outside, apply sunscreen with a high SPF, wear a hat, and put on sunglasses to shield your skin and eyes from UV radiation.

Make use of safe transportation

- Choose trustworthy, licensed providers while taking a taxi or other kind of public transportation. A visible identity badge and a meter to ensure a fair fee are standard in licensed taxis. Verify the driver and vehicle information if you're utilizing a ride-hailing service before boarding.

Bring the required documents

- Keep duplicates of your passport, government-issued identity, and other crucial documents in a safe place apart from the originals. Additionally, keeping digital versions on your phone or email for quick access is an excellent idea.

Ask for medical help if necessary

- There are medical facilities and pharmacies in Salamanca in case of any health issues or emergencies. Learn where they are and make sure you have travel insurance that includes medical coverage for the duration of your stay

Observe etiquette and customs in your area:

The local traditions and customs should be respected when in Salamanca. When visiting holy sites, dress modestly, obey regional customs, and be aware of noise levels, particularly late at night in residential areas.

Know the local emergency phone numbers

- Including the police, ambulance services, and your embassy or consulate, save the local emergency contact numbers in your phone. You'll be prepared for an emergency by having the information you need close at hand.

You can explore Salamanca with confidence and thoroughly immerse yourself in the city's rich culture, history, and energetic environment by following these safety and health recommendations. Make the most of your amazing trip to Salamanca by staying safe, looking after your health, and being careful.

Daily budget tips

Establishing a daily budget is essential when making travel plans to Salamanca so that you can fully take advantage of everything the city has to offer without going over budget. Here are some useful suggestions to assist you maximize your funds as you tour this alluring Spanish location.

Accommodation:

- Salamanca provides a selection of lodging choices for different price ranges. Think about booking a room at a hostel, guesthouse, or apartment that is affordable and comfy. To locate the finest bargain that matches your interests and budget, do some research and compare costs.

Dining:

- Salamanca has a thriving food scene where you may enjoy delectable Spanish food without breaking the bank. Find regional cafés and tapas bars where you may eat at reasonable prices and with authenticity. In restaurants, choose the "menu of the day," which offers a fixed-price meal with multiple dishes.

Markets and fast food:

- Investigate Salamanca's neighborhood markets and street food vendors for a tasty gastronomic experience on a budget. Enjoy inexpensively priced classic delights, locally sourced food, and freshly cooked snacks. A fantastic spot to enjoy a variety of regional flavors is the Mercado Central.

Transportation:

- A great method to discover Salamanca's small city center is on foot. You can save money on transportation expenditures by walking to the majority of the key attractions. Additionally, think about hiring a bike to get around the city and find its hidden gems while taking in the beautiful scenery.

Free activities and attractions:

- Salamanca has a number of free activities and sights that let you fully experience the city's culture and history without having to pay any money. Visit the city's magnificent churches, stroll quietly along the Tormes River, and explore the Plaza Mayor. For free concerts, exhibitions, or festivals taking place while you are there, check the local calendar of events.

Discounts and passes for museums:

- Invest in a tourist pass or cheap tickets if you intend to visit several museums and sites. You may save money while learning about Salamanca's rich cultural past by purchasing one of these passes, which frequently provide discounted entrance to numerous attractions.

Tap water:

- It is unnecessary to purchase bottled water in Salamanca because the city's tap water is of great quality. Bring a reusable water bottle with you, and whenever you need to satisfy your thirst, fill it up at the faucet.

Organize your time:

- To prevent impulsive purchases, do your research and have a strategy for your day. Find out whether there are any special offers or discounts on tourist sites, guided tours, or cultural events. You can make informed decisions and allocate your budget properly if you prepare in advance.

Toy shops in the area:

- Consider visiting local markets for one-of-a-kind and inexpensive keepsakes of your vacation rather of purchasing souvenirs from touristic shops. These markets provide a large selection of handicrafts, artisanal goods, and locally produced goods that capture Salamanca's spirit.

You may make your money go further while enjoying Salamanca's charm and beauty by adhering to these daily budgeting recommendations. Keep in mind that you can travel enrichingly and with lasting memories without breaking the bank. Keep an eye on your spending and make the most of your trip while having fun in Salamanca.

Local Customs and Etiquette

- To respect the city's culture and its citizens, it is imperative that you get familiar with local customs and etiquette before visiting Salamanca. Here are some helpful hints to assist you negotiate social conventions and leave a good impression while you're there.

Greetings:

- Salamanca residents value courteous greetings. The conventional way to greet someone when you first meet them is with a handshake. Maintain eye contact and adopt the proper formality for the circumstance. A warm "Hola" (hello) or "Buenos das" (good morning) is often appreciated in less formal contexts.

Dining manners:

It is usual to wait until everyone is seated before beginning the meal when dining in Salamanca. Be prepared for unhurried eating experiences because Spanish dinners can linger longer than in some other cultures. To show appreciation for the cuisine, it is polite to taste a little bit of everything on your plate and finish your meal.

Tipping:

- In Salamanca, tipping is customary. Although it's always welcomed to round up the amount, it's traditional to leave tips in restaurants of about 10% of the cost. Rounding up or leaving tiny change is acceptable at bars and cafés. Before leaving a tip, remember to confirm that the service fee has already been deducted.

Siesta customs

- Like many Spanish cities, Salamanca supports the siesta custom. Some stores and companies can close throughout the afternoon for a while. Consider this cultural custom when planning your activities. Take advantage of this opportunity to unwind, stroll slowly, or indulge in a quick nap.

Dressing code

- Although Salamanca has a laid-back and informal vibe, it's still vital to dress appropriately, especially when going to formal events or religious places. To show respect for the religious traditions, make sure your clothes covers your shoulders and knees before entering churches, cathedrals, or other places of worship.

Language:

- Although English is widely spoken in Salamanca, it will be appreciated if you make an effort to acquire a few fundamental Spanish words and phrases. Say "Hola" to people in the neighborhood and "Gracias" (thank you) when you get help or a service. Positive interactions can be greatly facilitated by being polite and being willing to speak a little bit of Spanish.

Punctuality:

- Being fashionably late is to some extent acceptable among Spaniards because of their more laid-back attitude toward time. To be on time for appointments, meetings, and scheduled tours is preferable. Respect the scheduled time, and it's polite to let the other person know if you expect to be late.

Public conduct:

- Salamanca has a dynamic atmosphere and is a thriving city, however it's vital to observe public behavior. As a courtesy to the neighborhood's residents and other visitors, try to limit your exposure to loud noise, especially after hours. Keep the city's cleanliness and attractiveness intact by being aware of your surroundings and avoiding littering.

You'll enjoy Salamanca more authentically and learn more about the city by adopting the regional customs and manners. Making lasting memories and developing friendly relationships with the residents of this amazing city will be facilitated by exhibiting respect for the local way of life. Enjoy your stay in Salamanca and get to know the city's distinctive traditions.

Emergency Phone Numbers

It's crucial to have access to emergency services while touring Salamanca in case something unexpected happens. To protect your safety and well-being while visiting the city, familiarize yourself with the following emergency numbers:

Police:
- Dial 091 to contact the neighborhood police in the event of any criminal activity, an emergency, or if you need quick assistance. They will react quickly and offer the required assistance.

Emergencies in Medicine:

- Call 112 for an ambulance if you or someone nearby needs urgent medical assistance. To ensure you receive the proper care, the operators will connect you with the right medical services.

Emergency Services:

- Call 112 for assistance if there is a fire or other emergency requiring rescue services. To manage the issue, the fire and rescue crew will be sent right away to your place.

It's important to keep in mind that you can call these emergency numbers from any phone, including a mobile phone, anywhere in Salamanca. When chatting with the operator, be ready to give precise details on your location and the emergency at hand.

It's also a good idea to find out about the hotel's internal emergency protocols and contact details if you are staying there. They can offer further direction and assistance in times of need.

While knowing the emergency numbers is crucial, it's also crucial to be cautious and take precautions to safeguard your safety. When exploring the city, be aware of your surroundings, heed any safety instructions, and use common sense.

Although Salamanca is a safe place to visit, it's always a good idea to be ready. You can feel secure throughout your stay by being aware of the emergency numbers and how to get in touch with the appropriate authorities. Never hesitate to call the right number in the event of an emergency, just remember. The neighborhood emergency services are there to help you and make sure you're okay.

Money and Currency Issues

To have a comfortable financial experience when visiting Salamanca, it's crucial to become familiar with the local currency and financial issues. Here are some helpful hints and details to help you deal with currency exchange and properly manage your money:

Currency

The Euro (€) is the country's legal tender across Spain, including Salamanca. To have local cash on hand when you arrive in Salamanca, it is advisable to exchange your currency to Euros beforehand. You can also use your debit or credit card to withdraw Euros from any of the city's ATMs.

Rates of exchange

It is advised to check the rates before exchanging your money because exchange rates sometimes vary. Banks and currency exchange companies can give you the most up-to-date exchange rates so you may convert your currency with confidence.

Change of Currencies

There are many banks and exchange offices in Salamanca where you may change your money. Banks typically provide competitive exchange rates, however they might only be open during certain hours. On the other side, exchange offices might operate on a more flexible schedule, including on weekends. Before deciding where to exchange your currency, compare rates and costs.

Using credit cards and ATMs

There are many ATMs in Salamanca that accept foreign credit cards. Before traveling, make sure your card will function abroad by contacting your bank to find out if there are any additional charges for using your card abroad. Although most hotels, restaurants, and stores now accept credit cards, it's still a good idea to have extra cash on hand in case a smaller business only takes cash payments.

Security and Safety

Make the required preparations to protect your assets and money. Keep your money, cards, and critical papers safe; ideally, in a hotel safe or a covert money belt. When using an ATM in a public setting, exercise caution and cover your PIN entry.

In order to prevent any potential problems with your cards being restricted for suspicious behavior, remember to advise your bank or credit card issuer about your vacation intentions, including your destination and travel dates.

You can have a trouble-free financial experience when visiting Salamanca if you are knowledgeable about the local currency, exchange rates, and money management advice. Enjoy your trip and make the most of your time by visiting the city's attractions, dining there, and taking advantage of all the exciting things it has to offer in terms of culture and experiences!

Useful Phrases

While visiting Salamanca, it can be helpful to learn some basic phrases in Spanish to enhance your communication and interactions with the locals. Here are a few useful phrases to assist you during your time in the city:

Greetings:

"Hola" (OH-lah) - Hello

"Buenos días" (BWAY-nos DEE-as) - Good morning

"Buenas tardes" (BWAY-nas TAR-des) - Good afternoon/evening

"Gracias" (GRA-see-as) - Thank you

"Por favor" (por fa-VOR) - Please

Asking for Help:

"¿Habla inglés?" (AH-blah een-GLAYS) - Do you speak English?

"¿Puede ayudarme?" (PWAY-de a-yoo-DAR-may) - Can you help me?

"Necesito ayuda" (ne-SE-see-toh a-YOO-dah) - I need help.

"Perdón" (per-DON) - Excuse me, pardon me.

Ordering Food and Drinks:

"Una mesa para [número de personas]" (OO-nah MAY-sah PA-ra [NOO-meh-ro de per-SO-nas]) - A table for [number of people].

"Quisiera pedir..." (kee-see-EH-rah pe-DEER) - I would like to order...

"La cuenta, por favor" (la KWEHN-tah, por fa-VOR) - The bill, please.

"Un café, por favor" (oon ka-FAY, por fa-VOR) - A coffee, please.

Getting Around:

"¿Dónde está...?" (DON-de es-TAH) - Where is...?

"¿Cuánto cuesta?" (KWAHN-to KWAY-stah) - what is the price?

"¿Puede llamarme un taxi?" (PWAY-de ya-MAHR-may oon TA-ksee) - Could you please call me a cab?

"¿Cuánto tiempo tarda en llegar a...?" (KWAHN-to tee-EM-po TAR-da en yeh-GAR a...) - What is the travel time to…?

Emergency Situations:

"Ayuda" (ah-YOO-dah) - Help!

"Necesito un médico" (ne-SE-see-toh oon MEH-dee-ko) - I need a doctor.

"Llame a la policía" (YA-meh a la po-LEE-see-ah) - Call the police.

"Estoy perdido/a" (es-TOY per-DEE-doh/ah) - I am lost.

Learning and using these basic phrases will show your respect for the local language and culture and can make your interactions more enjoyable. Don't be afraid to give it a try, as the locals appreciate the effort, even if your pronunciation isn't perfect. Enjoy your time in Salamanca and embrace the opportunity to immerse yourself in the local language and customs!

CHAPTER 1 0

Salamanca's travel itinerary

3 Days great itinerary

Day 1: Exploring Salamanca's Historic Charm

Breakfast:

- In the area of Plaza Mayor, have a delicious breakfast to start your day. Enjoy Spanish tortillas, freshly baked croissants, and a cup of flavorful coffee.

Lunch:

- Enjoy a tapas bar lunch the traditional way in Spain. Try several small meals like patatas bravas, gambas al ajillo, and pulpo a la gallega, which is octopus cooked in the Galician style.

Dinner:

- Enjoy a comfortable dinner at a nearby establishment that specializes in regional cooking. Enjoy meals like ternera de vila (Avila beef) and cochinillo asado (roast suckling pig).

Day 2: Cultural Highlights and Culinary Delights

Breakfast:

- At a delightful bakery, begin your day with a leisurely breakfast. Enjoy some freshly baked pastries, toast with tomato a la Spanish, and a cup of decadent hot chocolate.

Lunch:

- Visit a typical Mesón for a culinary adventure. Enjoy robust delicacies like Bacalao a la Vizcana (basque-style codfish) and Fabada Asturiana (Asturian bean stew).

Dinner:

- Visit a restaurant close to the riverfront for a great evening. Enjoy imaginative cuisine that combine classic Spanish flavors with cutting-edge cooking methods.

Day 3: Getting to Know Salamanca's Neighborhoods

Breakfast:

- At a café with outdoor seating, start your day with a delicious breakfast. Enjoy a warm cup of café with leche, a freshly squeezed orange juice, and a Spanish omelet.

Lunch:

- Visit the nearby village of La Alberca for the day to sample the local food. At a classic Mesón, enjoy a homey lunch while indulging in specialties like roast lamb or migas (breadcrumbs with sausage and peppers).

Dinner:

- Go back to Salamanca and have dinner at a spot renowned for its fusion food. Discover a special fusion of Spanish and foreign cuisines, enhanced by a carefully chosen wine list.

You may fully experience Salamanca's rich history, cultural legacy, and culinary delights with the help of this three-day tour. Feel free to further alter it to suit your preferences and take part in additional excursions or activities while you are there.

7-day fantastic itinerary

Day 1: Arrival and orientation

Breakfast:

- In the city's core, have a leisurely breakfast to start the day. Take pleasure in some freshly baked pastries, Spanish cheeses, and a cup of fragrant coffee.

Lunch:

- Lunch at a typical Spanish restaurant is a great way to learn about the regional food. Enjoy foods like Spanish omelets, gazpacho, and paella.

Dinner:

- Spend a special evening with friends at a restaurant close to Plaza Mayor. Try regional favorites like salted cod or roast lamb, such as cordero asado.

Day 2: Cultural treasures and historical landmarks

Breakfast:

- Visit a café for a classic Spanish breakfast. Enjoy churros con chocolate, a delicious and decadent breakfast food.

Lunch:

- Visit a restaurant close to the Salamanca Cathedral for lunch after taking a break from exploring. Try local fare like cocido maragato (traditional stew) or lechazo asado (roast suckling lamb).

Dinner:

- As you eat at a bustling tapas bar, take in Plaza Mayor's energetic environment. Try a variety of tapas, such as tortilla espaola, boquerones fritos, and jamón ibérico.

Day 3: Visit to Villa
Breakfast:

- For a quick breakfast you can have on the go, stop by a bakery. A cup of coffee and a variety of freshly baked pastries are available.

Lunch:

- Visit the quaint streets of Vila and eat lunch at a neighborhood eatery. Enjoy regional dishes like judas del Barco (local white beans) and chuletón de vila (grilled beef sirloin).

Dinner:

- Visit a traditional Mesón for dinner when you get back to Salamanca. Savour roasted meats while sipping a superb Spanish wine.

Day 4: Cultural Wonders and Stunning Works of Art
Breakfast:

- At a café close to the university district, start your day right with a full breakfast. Take pleasure in a Spanish-style omelet, tomato toast, and a hot cup of coffee.

Lunch:

- Visit the Casa Lis Museum of Art Nouveau and Art Deco and eat lunch there. Enjoy a quick meal while taking in the magnificent collection of artwork and design.

Dinner:

- Dine in a place with a creative atmosphere and top-notch cuisine. Enjoy creative dishes with artful presentations that are influenced by regional ingredients.

Day 5: Segovia day trip

Breakfast:

- At a café close to the Roman Bridge, take your time eating breakfast. Take pleasure in classic Spanish breakfast dishes like tostadas with tomate and a cup of café con leche.

Lunch:

- Visit Segovia's lovely streets and enjoy lunch at a typical mesón. Try the delicious Judiones de La Granja (white bean stew) or the renowned cochinillo asado (roasted suckling pig).

Dinner:

- Go back to Salamanca and have dinner at a hip spot that combines Spanish and other global flavors. Enjoy cutting-edge cuisine coupled with regional wines.

Day 6: Scenic Beauty and Gastronomic Delights

Breakfast:

- At a café by the river, start your day right with a nutritious breakfast. A variety of freshly squeezed juices, yogurt with granola, and herbal tea are also available.

Lunch:

- Take a culinary journey and have lunch outside of Salamanca at a classic rural establishment. Enjoy hearty fare such as roasted suckling lamb, wild mushroom risotto, and regional artisan cheeses.

Dinner:

- When you go back to Salamanca, have dinner at a hip spot with cutting-edge fare. Consider ordering the chef's tasting menu, which features the finest seasonal and regional ingredients presented in imaginative and artistic ways.

Day 7: Relaxed and Goodbye

Breakfast:

- Visit a café with outside seats and take your time eating breakfast. Enjoy freshly baked croissants, a selection of Spanish hams and cheeses, and a cup of fragrant coffee as you soak up the morning sun.

Lunch:

- Take a stroll through Salamanca's old town on your final afternoon there, and stop by a neighborhood bodega for a wine sample. Select appetizers like olives, Spanish tortilla, and marinated anchovies to go with the wines.

Dinner:

- Choose a classic Mesón that captures the spirit of Spanish food for your last meal in Salamanca. Enjoy a feast of grilled meats, seafood paella, and classic sweets like flan or crema catalana.

This suggested schedule is provided to assist you in making travel arrangements to Salamanca. Feel free to change it to suit your tastes and the hours that attractions and restaurants are open.

CONCLUSION

A genuinely lovely trip experience can be had in Salamanca. This Spanish treasure enchants tourists from all over the world with its stunning cathedrals, historic university, vibrant festivals, and lovely streets. we've looked at Salamanca's numerous features and given you in-depth analysis and suggestions so you may get the most out of your trip. Salamanca has something to offer everyone, whether you're a history buff, an art connoisseur, a foodie, or just looking for a nice retreat.

Explore the majestic Salamanca Cathedral and the historic Salamanca University walls to fully immerse yourself in the city's intriguing history. Take a stroll around the Plaza Mayor's charming streets while you take in the vibrant atmosphere and stunning architecture.

Enjoy the flavors of Salamanca by indulging in the regional food, which ranges from savory tapas to classic Castilian dishes. Find unique treasures to treasure in local markets, boutique stores, and artisanal craft shops by exploring hidden jewels in these places.

Through its celebrations and events, such as the Semana Santa and the Festival Internacional de las Artes de Castilla y León, Salamanca invites you to experience its vivid character. Immerse yourself in the regional traditions and customs while interacting with Salamanca's friendly residents.

The ideal time to travel, important practical information, and the numerous transit alternatives available to tour the city and its surroundings should all be taken into account when you plan your trip.

This book has given you a well-rounded plan to make the most of your time in Salamanca, whether you're staying a few days or a week. We hope that our guide has inspired and directed you to make priceless moments in Salamanca, from the must-see sights to the hidden jewels.

Pack your luggage, embrace your sense of adventure, and travel to Salamanca for a unique travel experience where history, culture, and beauty come together. Salamanca is waiting for you, eager to charm and enthrall you at every turn.

Recommendation

Every traveler can find something to do in Salamanca. Here are some major justifications for why we heartily endorse a trip to Salamanca:

Rich history

Explore Salamanca's historical sites and immerse yourself in centuries of history. You'll be transported back in time and have a deeper understanding of the city's cultural legacy as you visit the magnificent Salamanca Cathedral and the historic Salamanca University.

Amazing architectural feats

Observe the city's exquisite Gothic and Renaissance buildings. A few of Salamanca's architectural wonders are the Universidad de Salamanca's elaborate facade, the Plaza Mayor's opulence, and the charming Casa de las Conchas.

Cultural Activities

To really experience local culture, schedule your visit around one of Salamanca's bustling festivals or events. Experience Semana Santa's solemn processions or take in the creative performances at the Festival International of Castilian Arts. These occasions provide a rare window into Salamanca's heart and soul.

Foodie Pleasures

Enjoy the mouthwatering flavors of Salamanca's cuisine. The city's restaurants and pubs provide a wide variety of culinary delights, from delectable tapas to classic Castilian cuisine. Don't pass up the opportunity to try regional delicacies like hornazo, queso de Arribes, and jamón ibérico.

Charming Ambience

Take in the beautiful ambience as you stroll through Salamanca's constrained, cobblestone alleyways. You'll feel right at home in the city thanks to its lively plazas, busy markets, and quaint cafés.

A day trip

Use Salamanca's advantageous location to your advantage and visit the neighbouring towns and cities. Vila, Segovia, and Zamora are just a few destinations that make for enjoyable day visits and each has its own distinctive attractions and cultural experiences to offer.

Pleasant Hospitality

Salamancans are renowned for being hospitable and friendly. Your vacation experience will be enhanced by the eagerness of locals to impart their expertise and enthusiasm for their community.

When making travel arrangements to Salamanca, make careful to research the various lodging options, decide on the ideal time to visit, and map out your itinerary. Salamanca is a city that promises to be a wonderful travel destination and leave you with enduring memories thanks to its abundance of sights, cultural experiences, and culinary pleasures.

So gather your belongings, travel to Salamanca, and allow the city's beauty, history, and lively character to enchant you. With the help of this travel guide, you may discover Salamanca's hidden gems and have a trip you won't soon forget.

Enjoy your trip!

Printed in Great Britain
by Amazon

25396329R00106